ANOTHER

MANIFESTO

OF A

MADMAN

FOR GOOD

BY: JAY SHERMAN

ANOTHER

MANIFESTO

OF A

MADMAN

FOR GOOD

Unrelenting Positivity

Author: Jay Sherman

ISBN: 978-0-578-11018-9

I DEDICATE THIS NEXT MANIFESTO OF MINE TO THAT INNER VOICE INSIDE US ALL THAT BEGS US TO THROW AWAY OUR PETTY DIFFERENCES AND MEANINGLESS DISTRACTIONS SO WE CAN UNITE AROUND LOVE, HUMANISM, ACCOUNTABILITY AND WHAT WE ALREADY KNOW WE AGREE ON.

ACKNOWLEDGEMENTS

4/16/12 – 11:42am

ANOTHER MANIFESTO OF A MADMAN FOR GOOD

Thank you Mom for supporting me in all my ventures, teaching me to fill my own cup, and for proving that feeling gratitude on a daily basis is the way to true happiness. Thank you Pop for being the supportive, loving and determined example of what all "DADS" not "FATHERS" should strive to be; thank you for always pushing me to my full potential. Thank you Uncle Garry for always being proud of who you are, and always finding enjoyment in the lighter side of life. To Uncle Eugene for always taking a genuine interest in me and asking questions out of an authentic want to know the answer. Thank you Aunt Lisa for being a strong example of the potential a woman has to positively affect the lives of all the people around her. Thank you Grandpa Herman for your courage in making a better life for yourself after overcoming unimaginable obstacles, you have impacted my life more than you will ever know. Thank you Grandma Yona for breathing a sense of culture and a feeling of who I am into my life, my understanding surely wouldn't be the same without it. To Grandpa Mel for leaving me with one of my happiest childhood memories, I miss you a lot. To Grandma Laurine for having the balance of strength and love that should be a goal for many of us to strive to, especially me! Thank you Cousin David for taking a genuine interest in my writing, asking pertinent questions and showing that people with opposing views can agree on a lot more then they think they can.

Thanks to Ryan for being the brother I never had and for always supporting my creativeness and pushing me to achieve the things I dream about. To Sean for being the other brother I never had and for "getting" how the world works; and even though your views can be dark or disagreeable from my own sometimes, we can always come to an understanding that real power comes from the people and alternatives are always possible no matter how set in stone they may seem. Thank you Mackey for always being there as a buddy, providing a good story and a laugh when I've needed one and showing not only that persistence pays off, but an understanding of who we are and where we came from can provide a blueprint for how we can make our lives better and everyone else's around us as well. Thank you Laurie for being my biggest fan and supporter; for being a well of positive thought, good energy and determination of what's possible when people look for and find what the truth can achieve. Thank you Jaime for being my other biggest fan and for being a beautiful, intelligent and caring woman, who has proven time and time again that authenticity and truth are how we find the roots to many of our problems.

Thank you Tim for being my oldest friend and most trusted confidante, and for always being there with a positive thought, good story and conscious truthful tidbit about how the world "really works." To Jess for being a strong, beautiful, courageous and intelligent woman whose monumental effort to breed positive change into you and your children's lives is beyond admirable; stay strong, and always remember the universe bends towards justice for those of us who are conscious enough to receive it. To Lucy for helping to solve all the world problems with me, for being my favorite person to go to a show with, and for being a shining example of how important it is to go after what you want in life; thank you for being my buddy.

To Lilly for going after what makes you happy and for balancing what's best for your kids and your own psyche, and for looking out for my best interest. Thanks Lisa for not only being the best boss I've ever had and helping me to stay in this job for 4 years, but for giving me positivity when I'm feeling low, being a very supportive surrogate mom and for the life advice and pep talks about what I deserve in a woman. To Kayleen for being the sister I never had, for making me laugh, keeping up with me in the joke department, genuinely caring how my life turns out, and how I should and deserve to be happy. To Sara for being the perfect balance of beauty, intelligence, downright craziness, caring and self-esteem; and don't worry I still love you even if you forget your eyebrows ☺ To Dale for proving to me that somebody who runs a business and has employees can still be an authentic, caring person that never forgets how to have fun and try's to pass it on to everyone they come into contact with. To Randy for not only being interested in my work, but for being authentically interested in the issues it brings up. To John for loving life and for proving everybody should do the same. To Mark and Linda for always bringing me a smile, and for proving that no matter what path one may take in life, we always have a choice in our positive evolution if we do what our hearts tell us. To ECO LAB James who although we don't agree on everything, knows about how distractions can keep us down and how it's much better to start the conversation from where we agree than from where we don't. To the uniform guy for the good fish advice and stories, and for providing me a smiling face amidst a hard day's work. To Monte whose questions and genuine interest in my work have shown me that it is not only important to sing to people other than the choir, but people from opposing sides need to talk just as much or even more than people from the same sides.

Thank you to the Marsh for being my personal Walden Pond; the spot I can always count on as a peaceful refuge and place to reflect, for letting me be myself and for helping me to let go of the things that don't serve my highest good. To College Cove for providing me with the perfect example of everything a great beach spot should be.

Thank you for my life and to the world for providing me with challenges, heartbreaks, sorrows, adversity and painful memories, while at the same time providing the questions, answers, love, peace, light, lessons, priority importance and determination to overcome anything if I put my mind to it. Thank you for proving to me that the more thankful I am for what I have instead of being down on myself for what I don't, the more I will be provided with the answers to my questions, prayers and the culmination of my dreams.

THANK YOU, THANK YOU, THANK YOU!!!!

PROLOGUE

4/3/12 – 6:06pm

ANOTHER MANIFESTO OF A MADMAN FOR GOOD

Is it possible to change the political and social situation we are currently in? If we want to change our surroundings and make positive change for the world, how do we do it? We must learn when to fight and when to compromise, but how do we get there? If we get to the point where we say enough is enough and we feel in the deepest darkest depths of our soul we must do something, then what? How do we get to the point when everything doesn't feel like it's so locked in and set in stone? What pray tell is holding us back? Why does it seem like we're making the same mistakes over and over and over again while expecting different results and never learning anything? Are we insane?

We can get distracted by a lot in our daily lives, the bills, our spouse, our job, the state of the country and the constantly changing makeup of what used to be considered normal. Sometimes we get distracted by the little things. Sometimes it seems like we are so diametrically opposed to each other that we will never be able to agree on anything. We must ask ourselves, why is this? We must ask ourselves why we can agree 90% of the time, but it's those few and insignificant in the long run 10% of things that keep tripping us up.

These petty differences that we as a people keep getting caught up on and have a hard time dealing with, seem to prevent us from coming together to solve the things we need to solve. We can't unite and talk about what we don't agree on, which blinds us to the fact that we are able to work on the problems we can agree on. We concentrate on a few problems we can't get past, instead of concentrating on all the things we can. We start from a place of not agreeing so we get to a place where we do. We say there is this stuff we can't agree on, which prevents us from getting to the stuff that we can agree on. Doesn't this seem backwards to you? Doesn't it seem like it would much more effective to start the conversation from a place that we do agree?

Once we begin talking and treating each other like human beings because we realize we all have the same basic needs and wants and all come from the same basic place, we might have a chance to solve some of our ingrained and generational moral differences, or at least be able to sit in the same room as each other and be able to humanely discuss them like people.

MY MISSION AS A MADMAN FOR GOOD, AND IN PARTICULAR THIS SECOND INSTALLMENT AND CONTINUATION OF MY MANIFESTO IS DEDICATED TO STARTING THE COVERSATION FROM WHERE WE AGREE, AND THEN MOVING IT TO WHERE WE DON'T. LET'S GET TO WORK!!!!

ENTRY#51

9/26/11 - 2:29pm

ANOTHER MANIFESTO OF A MADMAN FOR GOOD

Are we a country that executes innocent people? Were we created as a union of United States so we could put to death anybody we want regardless of the evidence or lack thereof?

Was our court system put in place so we could give fair and equal treatment to all, or so we could let some people go free when there is no evidence or witnesses against them? Were the courts designed so that we would be able to keep a person locked up if the evidence or witnesses against them are proven wrong or false, and yeah I'll say it, even murder some people when there is no evidence or witnesses against them?

After a couple hundred years or so we seem to be reverting back to what introduced us to the need for a fair and equal "United States" in the first place. Maybe all the race and class attitudes that didn't change by the laws that were passed years ago but brewed under the surface, are currently showing some of us for the out front, ain't afraid to show it, blatantly racist bigots that we really are.

Or maybe because there are many positive social and political movements out there with a chance to really change things this time, those of us who have always controlled things are pulling out all the stops out of fear that our iron grip is slipping.

We can be a country that kills innocent people, or a country that saves innocent people, it is that simple.

I WILL ALWAYS REMEMBER THIS AS A MADMAN FOR GOOD!!!!

ENTRY #52

9/29/11 – 4:54pm

ANOTHER MANIFESTO OF A MADMAN FOR GOOD

Is there a reason we keep fighting and struggling towards authentic social justice? Is there something buried deep within our souls that screams out, "hey, get off your ass and do something. Because if you think you can just wait around for that magic bean to fall out of the sky that will fix every problem everywhere, you need to go back to school and learn something because you're going to be waiting a long time?"

To help us figure out our own personal path for change we could learn about the struggles that happened for the civil and human rights of all people, how they had to fight, claw, scratch out and hang on for every inch of progress they got. And you know what, they never gave up; even when things seemed impossible, when the deck was so stacked against them that they might as well not even show up at the table, they carried on, they persevered.

Some movements were successful in their pursuits and some were not, but that wasn't the point. The point is they fought (and in some cases died) for something they felt so strongly in their heart was the right and just thing to do, they had only one option, they had to stand up, stand tall and stand proud.

When it's all over for us, and all our earthly worries float away, the only thing left will be the personal relationships we made, the people we affected and the thought that we were the best human being we could be during our short time on this earth. We have a choice, nothing is set in stone and it's never too late for positive change until we say it's too late.

THIS IS WHAT I HAVE TO CONTINUE TO LEARN AND TEACH AS A MADMAN FOR GOOD!!!!

ENTRY #53

9/29/11 – 5:18 pm

ANOTHER MANIFESTO OF MADMAN FOR GOOD

If it's true that we are what we eat, is it also true that we might be what we create, destroy and/or dispose of as well? Do we have influence over the day's events and what happens in them, or are we just mindlessly walking around being controlled by some much bigger entity, zapping away any trace of free will?

Do we enter this mental state because we think some problems are too big, too hard, too much or too inconvenient to handle or do anything about so why should we even try?

The fact is, we do have the power, it is just some of us have been asleep, unwilling or unable to access this power for so long, that a little jog of our memory is in order.

The problems we face, especially the big giant ones that bombard us on a 24-7 365 basis make it seem like there is no way around them, but they aren't completely real; the fact is they only seem real because we put our faith in the idea that they are.

What would happen if we all started realizing that working together is much more productive than working apart? We might realize that to create peace, justice, love and harmony, we have to create it from within ourselves and everyone we personally come in contact with.

We have to be the change we want to see.

**I MUST INSTILL THIS EVERYDAY AS A MADMAN
FOR GOOD!!!!**

ENTRY #54

9/30/11 – 5:29pm

ANOTHER MANIFESTO OF A MADMAN FOR GOOD

Are we evolved enough as a species to know that the chains that bind us can be locked in by worldly influences and be self-inflicted at the same time? Is our collective consciousness at the point where we know we can't always change the worldly influences that cause bad stuff to happen, but we can always change our reaction to them? Do we come to the conclusion that all distractions that are placed on us we can never fully control, but we can render them useless and ineffective by completely ignoring them?

There will always be some of us that are under the assumption that full 100% control over our surroundings is possible. There might even be some of us that think full control over and distraction of the masses from what's really important is the only foolproof way to make the changes we seek.

What about the rest of us? Do we believe that once we throw off distractions by discounting and ignoring them, that we will render the powers that be useless? Are we willing to admit that we aren't perfect creatures and all have imperfections, but it's not those imperfections that drive us, and love is?

I HAVE TO FIGURE THIS OUT AS A MADMAN FOR GOOD!!!!

ENTRY #55

11/3/11 – 4:45pm

ANOTHER MANIFESTO OF A MADMAN FOR GOOD

Is organizing our priorities the way to accomplish what's really important in life? Is figuring out what deserves our time the key to positive social and political change? Have we always had the knowledge within us to produce a massive consciousness raising plan? Is this knowledge completely gone or just periodically gone when we need it?

If making a plan is the best way to accomplish something, where is our plan to usher in a new age of humanism and accountability? Do we need help designing it, or are the blueprints etched on our soul?

THIS IS ONE OF MY MOST IMPORTANT MISSIONS AS A MADMAN FOR GOOD!!!!

ENTRY # 56

11/15/11 – 10:28am

ANOTHER MANIFESTO OF A MADMAN FOR GOOD

When a social and/or political movement is building and looking to enlarge its numbers, how does it accomplish this very important, but very difficult task? Does it occupy a space with a message so pure and true that the majority of us (the 99%) will see its real world applications and out of a want to do good, will unite and throw off our oppressors?

Or does the movement's message of truth, justice and accountability fly so far and so deep in the face of the elite class that they (the 1%) must crack down harshly and exert their dominance over us so they can continue their grand illusion of control?

Obviously I don't know the full solution of how to build a thriving social and political movement or I would have built it by now. All I know is that politicians, corporations and all the other "money changers" that have woven themselves into our political system will only change for the positive when they feel their bottom line is being threatened. When this happens, they will exert immense pressure and sometimes violent means to suppress us or our demands.

This is when we have to come back in even stronger numbers. They will again try to suppress us. This is when we have to keep coming back and back and back until our numbers grow and grow and grow till they get that we're serious and in for the long haul, and can cause their way of operating to cease functioning. Let's go get em'. We are the 99%

THIS IS WHAT I MUST DO AS A MADMAN FOR GOOD!!!!

ENTRY #57

1/5/12 – 4:12pm

ANOTHER MANIFESTO OF A MADMAN FOR GOOD

Do we really ever know where our lives are leading? Can we decipher the rabbit hole at the same time we are going down it? Are we able to see all the things around us, while still being able to see what's ahead of us? If we see what's ahead, know what we want out of life and know where we want to go, is it ever guaranteed, or is it just implied if we put the work in?

The most we can expect out of life is that we put our best foot forward, that we tried our best and stayed true to the passion that burns within us. We can't always change what happens around us, but we can change how we react to it. Within this reaction however, it is imperative that we are thankful for what we have, so it can give us the motivation to achieve what we don't, not the other way around; that way we don't get stuck in that "woe is me" rut.

We might never know exactly where our life is going to lead, but we can steer it in a positive direction if we are thankful for what we currently have and work from there.

THIS IS SOMETHING I MUST REMEMBER AS A MADMAN FOR GOOD!!!!

ENTRY# 58

1/5/12 – 4:29pm

ANOTHER MANIFESTO OF A MADMAN FOR GOOD

Have the political winners in our current governmental makeup always been rich and always been powerful? Is running a city, county, state or country a position only for the rich and powerful? Are the day to day operations to much for the feeble minded commoner to handle? Are certain decisions made by the world's "power brokers" too in depth to be made by a normal human being? Is it possible a lower class, poor or poverty stricken person can form a thought big enough and broad enough that it would be universal among all people?

The event of the rich controlling the poor has been an aspect of every society since the beginning of time. We just have to remember that all of us considered "not rich" have always vastly outnumbered those of us considered rich, the 1% or the elite class. Change can only be achieved if all of us see what lies in front of all of us. We must never gloss over the true meaning of events. We must not see ourselves as cogs in a machine, but see ourselves as an awakening, a changing of the guard if you will.

THIS IS A DESIGN ISSUE OF SOCIETY THAT I MUST ALWAYS FIGHT TO FIX AS A MADMAN FOR GOOD!!!!

ENTRY# 59

1/5/12 – 4:44pm

ANOTHER MANIFESTO OF A MADMAN FOR GOOD

Are unconscious people always unaware of their actions? Do unthinking people act with purpose or do they really have no idea what they're doing or talking about? Do they think at all or do they just blindly follow whatever they're told, because what they hear makes perfect logical sense to them if they don't think about it? Are they aware at all? Or are these people just waiting for real truth to come from a source that lies to them at every opportunity? Does that make them insane, or does that put them at peace because they don't have to think?

We are more relaxed when we don't have to think because we don't have to leave our comfort zone. The difference is do we want to be at peace even though it might be a façade, ignorance drilled into us by forces with very sinister goals? Or should we accept some temporary pain as we uncover the truth so we can achieve a lasting, authentic, indisputable and honest peace in our soul; specifically because we think about it?

I MUST ALWAYS PONDER THIS AS A MADMAN FOR GOOD!!!!

ENTRY #60

1/5/12 – 4:57pm

ANOTHER MANIFESTO OF A MADMAN FOR GOOD

Are plans and procedures a fool proof way to stop anything bad from happening? Is making a decision or coming up with a scenario of possibilities a sure fire way to prevent disasters, or are there always variables we didn't think about?

Will our training say one thing, guiding us to act in a situation, then when something happens that makes our actions wrong even though we were only following the procedures we were taught, what then ? What if our training is wrong to begin with?

Figures of authority are supposed to be trained to handle crazy, unusual and sometimes violent situations; at least we hope they're trained for them. Sometimes they'll say things were beyond their control, and that their training is the guiding force in their decisions.

What if a kid comes to school with a grudge, punches a fellow student and proceeds into the hallway to cause more trouble. When the police (that happen to be at the school anyway) question him, he raises what looks like a semi-automatic handgun at them. They say drop it, he refuses, so they shoot and kill him; only to find out upon closer inspection of the body, that the gun was a non-lethal pellet gun and couldn't have killed anybody.

Does training or manuals account for what to do if we mistakenly shoot a kid for having a lethal weapon and find out later they were pointing a pellet gun at us, or do the rules and manuals themselves need to fundamentally change in design?

I HAVE TO FIGURE THIS OUT AS A MADMAN FOR GOOD!!!!

ENTRY #61

1/10/12 – 5:12pm

ANOTHER MANIFESTO OF A MADMAN FOR GOOD

Why do some of us think we can take advantage of others? Might we see the person or group as powerless and easily overtaken? Do we view them as unknowing and savage souls just waiting to be lifted up and out so they can grow and prosper? Or is it because when we are the aggressor it's because we're really insecure about ourselves, causing us to lash out because of our personal ignorance and unconscious attitude about who we perceive as a threat, which could be anybody? Maybe some of us are ignorant because we were never told to think for ourselves and were always given orders for every action we took. Maybe it's because we were abused and it's the only thing that's real to us.

Maybe our views are skewed so much to one side that anything that questions our thoughts, motivations and actions is viewed as a direct threat to us personally which we deal with by using overwhelming force; maybe we don't know any better. What we need to realize is that the world doesn't revolve around us, nor does it revolve around anybody else either. The sooner we realize our actions hurt us just as much as our victims, the sooner we will be at peace because we will see each other in ourselves

THIS IS WHAT I HAVE TO DEFEND AS A MADMAN FOR GOOD!!!!

ENTRY #62

1/13/12 – 9:38pm

ANOTHER MANIFESTO OF A MADMAN FOR GOOD

Is it hard for some of us to focus on what really matters? Do outside influences shield us from seeing what really drives us? Do we have so much bombarding us on a daily basis, entering the innards of our cortex from every direction that we don't know which way to go? Do we see ourselves as important enough in the bigger scheme of things to fight for what we believe in, and compromise when necessary? Or is it all of the above?

Maybe to gain focus we need to go out and struggle amidst adversity that we never experienced before. Maybe we need to step outside of ourselves so we can take a glimpse of what's to come. Maybe we need to take care of ourselves before we take care of anybody else.

Whatever the cause, label or reasonable assumption we want to give it, it can be hard to stay focused before, during or after we start along our path. We have to remember that no matter what, we must keep focused and moving forward or we'll get ran over. We must heal ourselves before we can heal the world.

THIS IS WHAT I HAVE TO CONSTANTLY REMEMBER AND CONTINUE TO REALIZE AS A MADMAN FOR GOOD!!!!

ENTRY #63

1/13/12 – 9:57am

ANOTHER MANIFESTO OF A MADMAN FOR GOOD

Can we be in tune with the moment even if that moment might be completely horrible? Are there coping mechanisms we use to tune out messages we may or may not see right in front of us? Is it possible that we could be completely misled by our thoughts, could they drive us in the wrong direction? Or could our thoughts, if focused and in tune, drive us in the right direction?

It's important to remember that coping and defense mechanisms can be safe havens for us during a certain situation, but can prevent our personal growth by denying what we really need in other situations. We must figure out what our priorities are, and that they are important enough to give credence to. Why do we seem to float around when all we want is to be grounded?

THIS IS VERY IMPORTANT IN REALIZING MY MISSION AS A MADMAN FOR GOOD!!!!

ENTRY #64

1/13/12 – 10:07pm

ANOTHER MANIFESTO OF A MADMAN FOR GOOD

If the big picture is out there for us all to understand, will we reach out and grab hold? Will we push it away because its volume is too immense for our tiny human minds to comprehend? Do we even realize it's there? Do we care? Or are we waiting for the right moment, when the time is just right to introduce out of the box and big picture thinking into our daily decision making? Is it too big a change for us to handle? Or are we just preparing for when all our little picture thinking comes to the forefront and we can't ignore it any longer?

We all feel the big questions, "Why am I here, where am I going" because they are part of the human experience. Things can get crazy out there in the world, but they are only crazy because we put our faith in them that they are crazy. If we're ready for this fight and truly want to build a winning strategy, we must, must, must pay attention and acknowledge the big picture, while never forgetting that it's the little things that make up life. We must balance our heart and mind within our body, so we can balance the heart and mind of the earth.

I MUST REMEMBER THIS FOR ALL OUR BENEFIT AS A MADMAN FOR GOOD!!!!

ENTRY #65

1/16/12 – 8:48am

ANOTHER MANIFESTO OF A MADMAN FOR GOOD

Is the reason important social and political messages can't reach those "hard to reach" people because the messenger isn't being authentic enough? Are those "hard to reach" people just unthinking and uncaring souls that run purely off emotion and zero off of critical thinking causing no amount of reasoning to do any good?

Do these people know exactly what they're doing when they seem to not be swayed by any kind of logical argument, because they are actually waiting for a nugget of truth that will reach them? Are they fake people trying to survive with ignorance and un-intellectualism?

Or are they so real a people that they can see through all the political ooze and goop that fogs up the landscape, and can tell it's not real?

When we are trying to reach somebody and persuade them to agree with a certain point, being real is the only way to truly succeed. We could be talking to a crazy uncle who doesn't think the crazy "Dems" or the crazy "G.O.P." are the key.

What about our cousin that contributes to any crazy cause that comes before them? What about our mom or dad that can't see past their own prejudices?

We might not be able to reach everybody, but if we're honest, down to earth and real, they will take us seriously, and they will listen not just hear us.

THIS IS A CONVERSATION STARTER I HAVE TO REMEMBER AS MADMAN FOR GOOD!!!!

ENTRY #66

1/17/12 – 7:45am

ANOTHER MANIFESTO OF A MADMAN FOR GOOD

Can we get our point across without judging the person we're talking to? Can we be passionate and pointed in our point of view, but not mentally judge who we're speaking with? If people with 2 diametrically opposed opinions have a discussion, will they always judge the others views as "just another liberal" or "just another conservative"? Will they be able to find the common ground they have, and figure out all the distractions placed on them (that exist to keep them from finding common ground) so they can unite and fight their common enemy?

Events and people seem so polarized today with radicals coming out on all sides of the political spectrum unwilling to compromise their position. When we're uncompromising, we are judging what the other side will do, we think their too crazy or too far out there; this is exactly what the people at the top want us to do. They want all of us to judge and fight each other, so we don't unite and fight and judge them. The bottom line, judging is not the way to reach people and find common ground, it is a way to distance ourselves from them. Do we want to unite and fight our true and common enemy? Can we stop judging each other long enough to get there?

THIS IS ONE THING I HAVE TO REMEMBER AS A MADMAN FOR GOOD!!!!

ENTRY #67

1/17/12 – 8:03am

ANOTHER MANIFESTO OF A MADMAN FOR GOOD

Have politicians always lied to our faces? Have they always said whatever the voters wanted to hear without a second thought about the implications of their numerous lies; is this consciously done with many sinister evil deeds planned behind them? Are we lied to by politicians who are just as dumb, judgmental, elitist, crass, smart or crazy as the people who vote for them? Do politicians create us, or do we create politicians?

We complain that politicians don't know what they're talking about and how they always lie to us. Here's the rub, if politicians know they're lying to us and we know the politicians are lying to us, what gives? How can we expect not to get lied to, when we expect to be lied to? How can we ever gain the truth, if we know what we're hearing is lies, but feed into it anyway by just going along for the ride?

If we really want the ultimate truth that we feel in our souls to come before us, it has to start with us not lying to each other.

I MUST CARRY THIS WITH ME AS A MADMAN FOR GOOD!!!!

ENTRY# 68

1/17/12 – 8:17am

ANOTHER MANIFESTO OF A MADMAN FOR GOOD

Why am I fighting this fight as a madman for good? Is it to help people shake off their distractions? Is it to show people how to get past lies that are spewed at them daily from every direction? Do I fight for the people who control the tempo of the argument so they can bend it towards their every will and desire? Is it to clear my mind of distractions that hold me back from accomplishing what I know deep down in my soul to be true, so I can try to save the planet from countless, completely preventable and pervasive problems? Am I a madman for good because some people need help realizing their true worth and clearing away their own distractions so they can implement humanistic accountability; is it because by helping others, I am really helping myself?

Whatever the answer is, I will keep striving with a passion that burns like a wildfire within me for positive social and political justice and change. I must do my small part during my short time on this planet so that we all know what it feels like to be loved, and what it's like to be completely and utterly free.

THIS IS A MAIN GOAL OF MINE AS A MADMAN FOR GOOD!!!!

ENTRY #69

1/17/12 – 8:28am

ANOTHER MANIFESTO OF A MADMAN FOR GOOD

Is the amount of money spent on political campaigns going to keep spiraling out of control until someone finally stands up and says enough is enough? By vastly increasing the amounts being "legally" spent on running for office, does it pull those campaigns further and further away from the average person? Once a politician has spent a billion dollars on a campaign, is it possible for them ever to relate to a majority of their constituents, without always sounding like a complete shill to their big money people and corporate donors?

Is the best example we can find of income inequality getting worse is ourselves becoming worse off? It seems since our social and financial situations are getting worse, the people we put into office who make laws and regulations are getting so much worse to the point they think betting an opponent $10,000 or having a $500,000 bill at Tiffanies is normal, while hard working people who happen to get food stamps because they need a little extra help to make it are considered abnormal. The biggest travesty of it all is not the fact that not nearly as many people get food stamps as are eligible, but candidates talking, and talking and talking about how they'll fix the problems for the poor, when they'll really only fix problems for people who they feel have influence over them (i.e. big donors, or us when we all unite).

All we need to do is show the powerful in very large numbers that we're mad as hell and we're not going to take it anymore. Then we'll see who has influence over whom.

THIS IS A PLATFORM FOR ME AS A MADMAN FOR GOOD!!!!

ENTRY # 70

1/17/12 – 8:43am

ANOTHER MANIFESTO OF A MADMAN FOR GOOD

If a president were Christian would it matter? What if they were Buddhist, Hindu or Sikh would it matter? What about if they were Jewish, Muslim, or Native American would it matter? If they were atheist would it matter? If they came from a home that had 2 dads or 2 moms would it matter? What if a president was an orphan that was abandoned by their parents at a young age, what if they were loved by their millionaire parents and given everything they wanted, would it matter? What if they were black or white, Mexican, South American, African, Asian, European or Eskimo, would it matter? If they were a man or a woman would it matter? What if they were both? What if the leader of the so-called "free world" smoked, drank, gambled and/or visited hookers, would it matter?

What matters to us as a people, is it that our president has a religious creed, race, ethnicity or sexual orientation we agree with? Or is it what that president will do to bring us together and raise our consciousness, no matter what they look like or where they come from? This might be the key to finding enlightenment, peace and a world where we truly live up to our ideas and principles.

RACISM, SEXISM AND DE-HUMANIZATION WILL ALWAYS BE THINGS I FIGHT AGAINST AS A MADMAN FOR GOOD!!!!

ENTRY #71

1/18/12 – 7:57am

ANOTHER MANIFESTO OF A MADMAN FOR GOOD

If a person or a group contributes unlimited amounts of money to a political campaign, what's to stop them from taking people over, and controlling all their movements and actions? If such a "puppeteer" were to pull the right strings could they force a candidate to sing whatever tune they wanted, even it was detrimental to society? If a puppet master moves the strings, what happens to the little bits of brain that rumble around inside the head of the puppet? Can the puppet think for itself? Or would they be completely dependent on outside influences or "string pullers" to think for them, because they wouldn't be able to think a thought that's not, "how am I going to get this person to like me?"

Money can pollute politics, especially when unlimited amounts are allowed to be spent; this is a danger zone. With this windfall, not only does it pull people apart from each other politically, it gets them to believe in lies. The politicians know they're lying to the people, the people know the politicians are lying to them, so what gives? Since everybody knows that everybody else is lying, what is the alternative? Maybe we should stop listening to the loudest voice, and start listening to the truest.

THIS IS AN IMPORTANT MISSION FOR ME AS A MADMAN FOR GOOD!!!!

ENTRY #72

1/18/12 – 8:10am

ANOTHER MANIFESTO OF A MADMAN FOR GOOD

Does negative advertising work when trying to demonize an opposing side? Does inserting negative language into a diatribe add to the power it has in drawing people to it? Is it possible the people the diatribe is aimed at actually believe it deep down, but are just never able to bring it to the surface? Are people actually and actively trying to decipher the dirty cobwebs of our political system only to be swung around 180 degrees by the loudest and most well-funded voice? Or are people just robots that respond when people yell at them?

We as a people have to know that there are going to be lots of other people out there who want to persuade us to believe in a certain thing, act in a certain way or vote for a specific person. We can be bombarded on a daily basis by negativity. However, this negativity is just a smokescreen, an illusion if you will. The "power brokers" have to fog over the minds of the people because they have no real power or ideas, just a bunch of hot air.

There are positive ideas out there, with positive people pushing them. We must remain eternally vigilant to find these people before it's too late.

I MUST FIND THEM AS A MADMAN FOR GOOD!!!!

ENTRY #73

1/18/22 – 8:22am

ANOTHER MANIFESTO OF A MADMAN FOR GOOD

Does our religion or belief structure prevent us from achieving a certain office, standard or practice? Just because we might believe in a different god or goddess than somebody else, does that necessarily mean we would make our god reign supreme if we were elected to office, while all other versions of god were thrown in the trash heap? Are we scared of things we personally don't know anything about? Do we think if one thing changes, it will cause everything else to snowball, and the ensuing avalanche will completely cover us with something that is 100% different from our present situation? Is it all just ignorance of the unknown?

If we run for a high elected office, no matter what our religious background, we should listen to all other voices, and not expect an "avalanche" of opinions to fall on our heads. If somebody is Jewish, Muslim, Hindu, Buddhist, Sikh or any of the other vast amount of non-Christian religions out there and they try to get our vote, we should be open their ideas. If a Jew or Muslim got elected, it wouldn't mean they would tear down the white house Christmas tree and local churches, any more than a Christian would tear down a mosque, synagogue or temple. We must realize we are all in this together.

I MUST NEVER FORGET THIS AS A MADMAN FOR GOOD!!!!

ENTRY #74

1/18/12 – 8:35am

ANOTHER MANIFESTO OF A MADMAN FOR GOOD

Has this country evolved to a point where we could elect a woman president? Since we were the first western industrialized nation to elect a black man president, are we ready to take it the next step? Given all the horrible atrocities and thoughts that have plagued our racial history and unfortunately continue to bleed into our present, given all that we still elected a black president, are we ready to elect a woman? Are the anti-black thoughts that linger with some of us stronger than the anti-woman thoughts?

It's not now, nor has it ever been a contest between who has been degraded the most, and who has had the most violence committed against them; It's just in our overall worldly history, women have been put down since organized religion came on the scene and squashed all matriarchal goddess cultures thousands of years ago. Whether we are prejudice to some stuff, and not to others, it all deserves to be talked about openly and honestly. We as a society need to get to a point where we see each other as just people; and if one of us attempts to be the leader of the "free world", we need to judge them on their ideas, policies and platforms, not their gender, the color of their skin or where they came from.

I MUST REINFORCE THIS AS A MADMAN FOR GOOD!!!!

ENTRY #75

1/18/12 – 8:48am

ANOTHER MANIFESTO OF A MADMAN FOR GOOD

Honestly, what kind of changes would we like to see in this day and age? Would we like to win the lottery, get a new job, new car or a new life? Would we like to see our political system taken over by vultures looking to pick the bones clean reinforced by a deluge of amazingly well funded negativity meant to sway us from what we know is right? Would we like to see a government in place that actually works for all of us, instead of against most of us? Would we like to see a place where income equality is actually equal, where people of all sexes, races, creeds, ethnicities and sexual orientations are treated equally? Would we like to see a country where the well-funded smokescreen meant to distract us and keep us fighting amongst each other, doesn't have any power because we really know what lies behind it?

I think most of us would like to see a world more equal and fair to all its inhabitants, because we would have real opportunities to achieve greatness, not just the illusion of opportunities. For this to happen we can't just sit around and wait for it to fall in our laps; and although it might sound cliché, we must get out there and be the change we want to see. We are our best example.

THIS IS ONE OF MY MANY MOTIVATIONS AS A MADMAN FOR GOOD!!!!

ENTRY #76

1/19/12 – 4:03pm

ANOTHER MANIFESTO OF A MADMAN FOR GOOD

Is blatant hypocrisy blatantly obvious to everyone? When we see somebody in a position of power or authority make a decision or give a statement that fly's in the face of everything they've said before, can all of us see it?

When one of us says something that completely disproves a point we made previously, can all of us hear it? What if we support and laud a decision that states it supports one thing, but really tears it down, do all of us notice?

A clear skies act isn't supposed to allow more pollution by letting more waste into the atmosphere. A healthy forest initiative isn't supposed to clear cut a bunch of trees so development can take place.

A patriot act isn't supposed to take away the rights and freedoms that make us want to be a patriot in the first place. And certainly we are not supposed to stop an ethnic studies program because of "alleged" racial bias caused by hearing diverse voices, and then say in the same breath that we want more diverse voices in the classroom.

We can't say we want more opinions, and then stop those opinions from being heard because we say we want to be fair to all races by allowing a vast array of voices in.

Can everybody detect the big steaming pile of hypocrisy right in front of us? Maybe all of us should open our eyes and our noses, look around and take a big whiff.

I MUST DO WHAT I CAN TO END HYPOCRISY AS A MADMAN FOR GOOD!!!!

ENTRY #77

1/18/12 – 4:18pm

ANOTHER MANIFESTO OF A MADMAN FOR GOOD

If we start noticing all the blatant hypocrisy around us, does it sink in? Will the sheer magnitude of its invasiveness make mincemeat of our minds? Will it be too much for the average one of us to handle? Will it flip some of our worlds upside down, or will it be just a new beginning for us?

It's almost impossible to know how all of us would act or react in a certain situation, heck I don't even know how id react in every situation; but I do know how I would enter into a situation, and that's with an open mind. The key is to let previous judgments go, and come into the situation like we are viewing it for the first time, just from a different perspective.

Understanding different points of view is imperative when peace, justice, humanism and accountability are concerned. I'd bet that if we were given differing opinions and truly understood where they originated, the hypocrisy wouldn't be hard to comprehend because we would understand what motivated it. Finding the reasons to why things happen is the first step in finding out how they work.

I MUST CONTINUE TO LEARN THIS AS A MADMAN FOR GOOD!!!!

ENTRY #78

1/19/12 – 4:30pm

ANOTHER MANIFESTO OF A MADMAN FOR GOOD

Do elections in elementary school, junior high and high school differ from the way "adult" elections work? Are the popularity contests that permeate the school yard the same as the popularity contests that permeate the halls of congress? Is the reason somebody runs for office the same at any age, or is it more complex than that?

Adults come from somewhere, usually grown up from a child. Politicians weren't created in some laboratory somewhere by some alien witch doctor, they weren't conjured up by some genie or wizard with a magic wand; they weren't even placed in a given or wanted position because of their own choosing.

People who hold elected office are elected by those of us who may or may not know why we're motivated to vote for them; what we do know is we put people in high places. The people we elect are not foreign beings, they are us. Whether the voter is 8, 13, 16, 20 or 65, the fact remains that we elect people that are just like ourselves. People that are alike tend to be people, right? The funding for elections might evolve and change over time, but the motivation for voting, electing and running for office never will.

I MUST REMEMBER THIS ON MY JOURNEY AS A MADMAN FOR GOOD!!!!

ENTRY #79

1/19/12 – 4:46pm

ANOTHER MANIFESTO OF A MADMAN FOR GOOD

If we don't have an idea of where we'd like to be or go, how can we ever expect to get there? If we don't have a plan, (whether it be in our minds or written down) can we end up just floating around looking for purpose? If we don't focus on something worthwhile at an early age, can we still focus on it as we get older and are pulling on many more responsibilities? If we try to do too much, do we end up doing nothing at all?

There are so many things out in the world that could use some positive change, that it might seem overwhelming to us sometimes. The task is so large and there is so much to do, we might end up thinking about everything we can do all at once, causing our minds to spin out of control with all the possible actions we could take on any given day.

If we choose one path, or maybe a few, (depending on what we can handle) we will be able to focus on a goal, and then accomplish that goal; because accomplishing something positive is the goal, right?

I MUST REMEMBER WHATS REALLY IMPORTANT AS A MADMAN FOR GOOD!!!!

ENTRY #80

1/19/12 – 4:57pm

ANOTHER MANIFESTO OF A MADMAN FOR GOOD

When fighting for our rights or anybody else's, is it important we always ask ourselves why? Why is it important that we don't get taken advantage of? Is it okay if we earn a paycheck but pay a higher tax percentage then somebody who makes 1000x more money than us, and uses loopholes to get out of paying most of their taxes anyway? Why should somebody not get seen by a doctor or even be allowed to hold an insurance policy when they get sick? Why should all the power and money flow to the top, when all the cuts and sacrifices are flowing to the bottom? Why should the 1% tell the 99% what to do and how to live their lives? Why should somebody be labeled as lazy and dumb if they're poor or happened to be laid off from work? Why are votes cast for people who will rule against the masses at every turn? Why do bad things happen when the truth is told and the people at the top are exposed? Why don't we rise up, we are the majority after all?

We must know why, before we can ask how.

WHEN FIGHTING FOR JUSTICE, I MUST ALWAYS ASK WHY AS A MADMAN FOR GOOD!!!!

ENTRY #81

1/21/12 – 5:33am

ANOTHER MANIFESTO OF MADMAN FOR GOOD

When a dog whistle goes off, who hears it? Does a dog hear it because their owner is calling for them to come and eat their dinner? Do other animals hear it and come running? Does a voter hear the subtleties in it, and realize it's a signal for them to vote in a certain way? Is it a way of saying something without coming right and saying it?

We can't go around using the "n" word anymore, so we might use the words violent, scary, different, them or exotic. We might say forced integration or states rights. We might say welfare queen or food stamp president. We might even say blacks should demand jobs not handouts, as if no black person is working anywhere and only has the chance to work when a white person tells them it's okay to do so. We must get past all our past and present ugliness so we can have a better future.

When laws were passed "banning" institutionalized racism, (i.e. the 13-15 amendments, and voting and civil rights acts) it might have changed the law, but it didn't change some of our minds and opinions. We must stop using dog whistles to call bigots and racists to our sides, and start saying what we really mean. If we say what we mean, we can acknowledge it, and let it go.

I MUST NEVER FORGET THIS AS A MADMAN FOR GOOD!!!!

ENTRY #82

1/21/12 – 5:47am

ANOTHER MANIFESTO OF A MADMAN FOR GOOD

If we stop using dog whistles, coded language, and say what we really mean and feel in our hearts, will the world be better off? Will all the honesty let us as a society (or force us, depending on how we look at it) to grow and evolve, finally, after all these years because we will see where we have to improve?

Will all the blatancy filling the airwaves cause us to be disgusted and truly turn against the racist and bigoted thinking that has plagued our past, (as should be obvious to all by now) and also plagues our present? Would our non-evolved side see dog whistles as a chance to come out of the woodworks because of the potential for a much wider and receptive audience?

Being honest with ourselves about who we are and where we came from is never a bad thing; let me say that again, being honest with ourselves about who we are and where we came from is never a bad thing! Actions come from what kind of character we have and what kind of human being we want to be.

Do we want to continue all the mistakes of the past, and carry on with them as though nothing has happened between now and then? Do we want to disregard our mistakes all-together and forge a new path? Or should we look at the past, acknowledge it, let go what was detrimental to human kind, and continue on with what was beneficial so we can improve the lives of all humans?

I MUST REMIND PEOPLE OF THIS CONSTANTLY AS A MADMAN FOR GOOD!!!!

ENTRY #83

1/21/12 – 6:00am

ANOTHER MANIFESTO OF A MADMAN FOR GOOD

If we stop using coded language, take a look at who we are and what we would like to see for our children, can we talk about all that has plagued us in a civil and humanistic way? Would we be able to converse about touchy subjects that might raise our excitement levels, but would avoid delving into personal attacks? Can we talk about racism and how each race, scratch that, how each human should treat each other without judging who our family might have been, what group our brother might be affiliated with, or what we might think deep down and might not want to admit? Can we talk about racial issues without letting anything color our lenses causing us to judge? Or do we have to acknowledge all that and let it go?

We have to talk about where we came from, so we now where were at presently. We have to talk about where were at presently so we know where we're headed. Therefore, it is imperative we're aware of where we came from and what's around us so we have some control over where we're going. It's all about positive evolution not negative devolution.

THIS CONCEPT IS IMPERATIVE WHEN I START THE CONVERSATIONS AS A MADMAN FOR GOOD!!!!

ENTRY #84

1/12/12 – 6:13am

ANOTHER MANIFESTO OF A MADMAN FOR GOOD

If we talk about what went wrong in the past and what's going wrong in the present so we can create a better future, are we only looking at things from one angle? If we look at all the negative, does it help us realize what's positive? Do two wrongs make a right, do four, do eight, do 1,000, do a million? Do we have to look at all the bad times that existed and might still exist, balanced with all the good stuff so we can make a fair and informed decision?

Do we observe all the bad and all the good, let go of the bad and retain the good when we form our psyche? To get an accurate picture of a problem, we must get an accurate picture of the "whole" problem; we can't just gloss over what we don't like, but we also mustn't gloss over what we do like either. When an inspector goes to Guantanamo bay to check out the living conditions and interrogation procedures, and are only shown what the guards, government and military want them to see, they might think everything is all good; it is only when they are given complete access do they find out what's really happening. We must know ourselves, so we can really know ourselves.

I WILL ALWAYS CARRY THIS WITH ME AS A TEMPLATE ON MY MISSION AS A MADMAN FOR GOOD!!!!

ENTRY # 85

1/21/12 – 6:25am

ANOTHER MANIFESTO OF A MADMAN FOR GOOD

If we know our surroundings as much as humanly possible, what's the next step? After we've planned and planned and planned, then what? When or where is the next big idea or suggestion going to come from, an outside source or an inside source? We have this innate ability to be our worst enemy and our biggest cheerleader at the same time. We must learn that the more we know, the more we can't un-know. Once we've picked up the carpet to see what's been swept underneath, there is no going back. Once our eyes have been opened, there is no closing them. We must embrace the flow, power, humility, excitement, motivation and strength that comes from figuring out who we are in the larger sense and in the smaller sense. We must not get scared of its awesome power and size which might try to humiliate us into submission.

When we ask what the next step is, we should take everything we've discovered about how the world really works and use it for positive change. We shouldn't learn and find out stuff just to let it sit there doing nothing like money in a savings account. We learn it so we can use it. We know it so others can know it. We embrace it because it's the key to moving us forward as a human race.

I MUST NEVER FORGET THIS AS I EMBARK AS A MADMAN FOR GOOD!!!!

ENTRY# 86

1/22/12 – 9:29am

ANOTHER MANIFESTO OF A MADMAN FOR GOOD

I'm not sure who first said you got to give a little to take a little. I don't know who first came up with the idea of paying it forward, taking care of our neighbors or understanding what it means to be a human being.

I don't know who came up with those things, but you know what, it doesn't really matter; it doesn't matter who put it out there, it only matters that it's out there. Good thoughts, positivity, humanism, accountability and humility are all ideas that will lift our collective consciousness to a point where we'll wonder how we ever got along before. How we were able to tear each other down and how we were able to take advantage of a person's alleged inferiority will not be something that drives us. Once we realize that we have the same basic needs as everybody else, that we can make it through any problem using accountability of the responsible person and seeing each other as ourselves, there is nothing we can't accomplish as a species.

It won't matter where the ideas came from, it will only matter that they help to facilitate the positive and conscious evolution we all feel is possible.

I MUST HAMMER THIS HOME AS A MADMAN FOR GOOD!!!!

ENTRY #87

1/22/12 – 9:43am

ANOTHER MANIFESTO OF MADMAN FOR GOOD

Once we see each other as ourselves, are accountable and treat all beings as though we eat from the same trough, what's next? Once we have prepared, is it enough that we have conscious thoughts, or must we put them into action? Is thinking about doing the right thing or actually doing the right thing the end game? Is there an end game at all, or is it just about the journey? Is the reason it might be about the journey because the endgame is to complex and beautiful that we couldn't possibly understand it, at least not yet?

Thinking of the tough questions in life about materialism, the distractions placed on us that keep us from uniting and about the corruption from on high, bring us closer to nature. Knowing why we treat each other badly is half off the first step; our love for human kind and the earth, the way we take care of each other and the function of building up each other and not tearing each other down is the other half of the first step. Remember it may seem like a lot, but it is only the first step. The second and third steps will be up to us to create a positive progressive, not regressive plan to benefit us all.

I HAVE TO REMEMBER BABY STEPS ON MY MISSION AS A MADMAN FOR GOOD!!!!

ENTRY #88

1/22/12 – 9:56am

ANOTHER MANIFESTO OF MADMAN FOR GOOD

It's a blustery time to be human. The winds of change are blowing so hard, that sometimes a gust can blow us over. A tree branch might break and fall straight onto the path we thought we were going to take. Sometimes we think nobody feels the force of energy we are feeling.

Even though the wind might kick up, it's about how we react to it. The one thing we can be sure of is that the wind will blow no matter what we try to do to block it, it's a guarantee. We have to accept the fact that the wind will blow through from time to time just to keep us on our toes. We must ask ourselves, are we going to let the winds of change blow us down and apart, or are we going to have respect for them, because they keeps things fresh and have the potential to wipe the slate clean. Are we going to stand against change, or are we going to stand with it?

I MUST KEEP THIS ON THE FOREFRONT OF MY MIND AS A MADMAN FOR GOOD!!!!

ENTRY #89

1/22/12 – 10:07am

ANOTHER MANIFESTO OF A MADMAN FOR GOOD

If we know we must prepare and accept that change is going to come, then what? Do we keep deepening our understanding by loving our neighbor until the answers appear to us with extreme vibrancy? Should we keep fighting for what's right even though we might not see the light at the end of the tunnel? Can we keep persevering when and/or if the deck is completely stacked against us? Is it possible for one person to make a difference when the problems are so big and there seems to be many people on many opposing sides?; Is it also possible that this is exactly what the "power brokers" and "money changers" want us to think so it keeps us blind to what's really going on?

The "powers that be" want us to doubt ourselves and think were not strong enough, rich enough or smart enough to deal with our neighbor alone at the top; they want us to eat our bread and have our circuses, so we won't see them behind the curtain for the feeble and powerless people they really are. They tell us one person can't change the world, well if everybody thought that, nobody would ever change anything. If we all thought we could change the world, we would and we will.

I MUST REMEMBER THIS IS A CRUCIAL PART OF MY PLAN AS A MADMAN FOR GOOD!!!!

ENTRY #90

1/22/12 – 10:12am

ANOTHER MANIFESTO OF A MADMAN FOR GOOD

We all talk, we all think, we all act and we definitely all pretend on a daily basis. Life is an interesting dance with many confusing and complex steps set to music that nobody can fully understand. We are each other on a daily basis. The old saying that we are what we eat is also true about life; we get what we put into it. How do we sustain ourselves for the long haul so we're mentally able to keep putting our own energy into it? Is it different for every one of us, or is it basically the same, just slightly tweaked?

We are all just traveling along on our own personal journeys. We will have all sorts of different people come into our lives along the way that might only be there for a short period of time, even though we might have wanted them to stay longer. Also, we might have people come into our lives for a longer period of time who we definitely wanted to leave sooner. The great thing about this is we all serve a purpose. We all serve to teach a lesson we might have had to learn the easy way or one we might have had to learn the hard way. The point is we learn it, get over it, let go of the bad, keep the good, keep moving forward, keep achieving and keep loving. We must see each other as ourselves, so we can better the lives of all of us.

I MUST CONSTANTLY REINFORCE THIS WITHIN MYSELF AS A MADMAN FOR GOOD!!!!

ENTRY #91

1/24/12 – 6:48pm

ANOTHER MANIFESTO OF A MADMAN FOR GOOD

Does giving a speech provide the perfect platform for getting a certain point across in a way that everyone will be enthralled and hang onto every word? Does it provide the speaker with a way he or she can pretty much say anything they want without getting talked back to by people needing clarification on something they probably forgot they said anyway? Are speakers afraid of town hall meetings because anybody could stand up and say anything including questions that make them look dumb by proving they have no idea what they're talking about? Or does working from a script allow the evening to go off exactly as planned?

The last thing a candidate for public office wants is to be caught off-guard. They don't want to get caught looking stupid by not knowing an answer they should know, or unwilling to back up what they're saying because they never allow a follow up question to get through which would make them look like they aren't fully in control. Speeches might give the perfect platform for the speech giver, but not the audience when they aren't allowed to ask why.

THIS IS ONE OF THE THINGS I MUST FIX AS A MADMAN FOR GOOD!!!!

ENTRY #92

1/24/12 – 7:00am

ANOTHER MANIFESTO OF A MADMAN FOR GOOD

If it really is true that it's always darkest before the dawn, does it always have to be that way, has it always been that way? Why do we say things always get worse before they get better? Do things have to be broken and/or completely destroyed before we will wake up and realize that maybe the path we are going down isn't the right one? To make things a lot better or even make slight improvements does the whole slate need to be wiped clean?

The question really is, if the slate is totally wiped clean, would we really be changing or improving something, or would we be creating something totally new?

Sometimes new things have to be brought in to take out what doesn't serve us anymore. Some things need to be changed so it makes our lives better, easier and/or more fulfilling. But when a somebody or a group of somebody's start talking about wiping the slate clean, that's when we have to watch out for them. It might be the darkest before the dawn, but has it always been like that, does it always ring true, is the idea itself created to distract, or is it always an honest portrayal?

I MUST ASK MYSELF THIS AS A MADMAN FOR GOOD!!!!

ENTRY #93

1/24/12 – 7:15am

ANOTHER MANIFESTO OF A MADMAN FOR GOOD

Are we as humans, or should I say are we as creatures or mutants of our political system able to pick out hypocrisy when it comes up? Can we decipher it when it appears, even when it comes from somebody we support? Is hypocrisy more obvious when it comes from somebody we don't support, or do we just think it does because our views are skewed to the opposite side? Are we hypocritical when we go through our daily lives because we're human and aren't perfect? Is it even possible to live 100% by our principles? Would we even want to if we could?

We are not perfect beings. We aren't robots created with a predetermined purpose, so that our whole meaning in life is fulfillment of that purpose, and then we die. We have some say over our actions, we have free will. We all have choices. It all comes down to, "can we realize that everybody is a hypocrite by virtue of being human, just too varying degrees with different underlying purposes?" Can we take this knowledge to mean that different people learn in different ways? Can we fully realize that all of us are the same but totally different at the same time?

I MUST FIGURE THIS OUT FOR MYSELF AS A MADMAN FOR GOOD!!!!

ENTRY #94

1/24/12 – 7:29am

ANOTHER MANIFESTO OF A MADMAN FOR GOOD

When new knowledge and information comes in, (as it does to an exponential amount on a daily basis) how we process it can make all the difference. If somebody tells us something that we never heard, how should we react to our world being flipped around? Is there a way of being that would prevent this from happening? Is there a way for our ship not to get tipped over or smashed up when a giant wave of change comes; is there a way we can slice through it?

We all must get to a point where we expect change to happen; we won't know where or when, just that it will happen. Some people describe it as expecting the unexpected, but it's much more than that.

We must roll with what happens, because we can't always change what happens out there, especially when it's so big. Not that we can't make big changes, we can; it is possible, that's what this book try's to promote and then institute. We can't change everything, but we can change our reaction to it. This reaction will cause us to take action.

I MUST BUILD THIS UP SO IT'S PART OF OUR TOOL KIT ON MY MISSION AS A MADMAN FOR GOOD!!!!

ENTRY #95

1/24/12 – 7:40am

ANOTHER MANIFESTO OF A MADMAN FOR GOOD

As we enter into a new year, a new month, a new week, a new day, what will transpire to improve all our lives? What will be detrimental, what will be helpful? Do we have no say or no control over what happens?

Should a bank that is private from the government, tell the government what to do? Should there be government banks telling private businesses what to do? Should we be allowed to make money off of money so people without money in the first place don't know what's going on and will believe anything there told?

We are one people, one human race and one species. We must have a sense of togetherness and brotherhood no matter what end of the political spectrum we find ourselves on if we hope to accomplish the big changes all of us dream about. Once we figure out we're all differently the same, what transpires a minute, hour, day, month or year from now, we'll be ready. We will be standing together to destroy ugliness and end degradation.

I MUST REMIND EVERYBODY OF THIS INCLUDING MYSELF IF I TRULY WANNA BE A MADMAN FOR GOOD!!!!

ENTRY #96

1/25/12 – 7:44am

ANOTHER MANIFESTO OF A MADMAN FOR GOOD

If life is what we make it, are we working off some sort of recipe that tells us what to do along the way step by step? Do we just dive into life with reckless abandon, with no plan and just shoot from the hip while asking questions later? Or do we know what we're doing because we've seen other people fail horribly and fall flat on their faces, while others have succeeded so much they are still climbing to untold heights beyond their wildest dreams?

Maybe we enter life or many of its challenges with an idea of what's going to happen. Maybe we've seen a similar situation and where it worked out for someone, causing us to attempt that method. Maybe we know what to avoid and what to take in. Even if we know how to fail and how to succeed, it doesn't mean anything is guaranteed; life could just decide it wants to stop on a dime and go into a completely different direction.

We all have an idea of what life is about or where it's going even though it's constantly evolving and changing. We must remain vigilant and ready, for we know the changes are here and are going to keep coming. How we react to them is up to us.

I MUST REMIND MYSELF AND EVERYBODY ELSE OF THIS AS A MADMAN FOR GOOD!!!!

ENTRY #97

1/25/12 – 7:58am

ANOTHER MANIFESTO OF A MADMAN FOR GOOD

When somebody in a position of power or authority influences a decision, what is the real reason for their support? Do they have some evil plan meant to destroy a certain way of life by portraying it as evil, but say they just want to help the people help themselves? Maybe they're evil geniuses, planning and planning and designing and working until their plan to take over the world is complete? But what if they use that power and influence to bring on an admittedly positive outcome? What if they really are out to benefit society instead of tearing it down like so many caricatures have portrayed them as desiring?

Unless we know a person personally, we won't know what their real and honest intentions are; sometimes we still don't even if when we do know them personally. We could know somebody a long time and still not know why they do something. We must open our eyes and our minds to all the possibilities. A "power player" might mean to do the world harm, or they might want to heal the planet from its historic wounds. We will only know if we pay attention.

BEING VIGILANT AND ALERT IS ONE OF THE MOST IMPORTANT ASPECTS OF BEING A MADMAN FOR GOOD!!!!

ENTRY #98

1/25/12 – 8:10am

ANOTHER MANIFESTO OF A MADMAN FOR GOOD

When we fight amongst each other about our differences on a specific issue, is the divide too strong and too big to ever cross? When we are at each other's throats and it seems like we will never agree on anything, even the color of the sky, where do we go from there? When or if we see the other side as dumb and having no merits, how can we ever expect to agree? We have a lot of differences among us politically, religiously, racially, culturally and even sexually. Some of us are liberals, some of us are conservatives. Some of us are black, white, brown, red, yellow and all the other colors of the rainbow; some of us might even be gay. Yet despite what makes us unique as a human being, also makes up our character.

We must find out the real problems at the root of our societal ills. Some of us might think of it as just another liberal extending the welfare state, or just another conservative extending the police state, a religious person extending the moral debate, a certain culture expanding on racial problems or a person expanding on people's rights. We must realize that we and all other people around the world with all our differing characters all want to see a better world. Let's work together since we have the same goal anyway.

I MUST ALWAYS STAY AWARE AS A MADMAN FOR GOOD!!!!

ENTRY #99

1/25/12 – 8:24am

ANOTHER MANIFESTO OF A MADMAN FOR GOOD

If we are all trying to better the world with different methods because of our background and life experience, are we going to meet up in the middle like some crazy scavenger hunt? If we all take a singular, solo path towards what we feel in our hearts is right, how do we link back up with people if we are striving alone? If we all start at the same point, go off in different and sometimes completely opposite directions, how do we re-configure to fit in line with everyone else? How can we heal the world, if we are only looking to heal ourselves?

Fighting, striving or achieving something for a specific cause in a specific instance can be very beneficial to society; but when we ignore other ways to improve society because we believe ours is the best and only way, we grow apart.

Fighting for a cause is a great thing and it may save us all one day. When we focus on our similarities instead of our differences, we will see how our end goals are basically the same. Let's open our eyes, and feed our souls with compassion, connection and consciousness raising.

I MUST WORK VIGANTLY TO MAKE THIS A REALITY AS A MADMAN FOR GOOD!!!!

ENTRY #100

1/25/12 – 8:35am

ANOTHER MANIFESTO OF A MADMAN FOR GOOD

Have we ever wondered what would happen in this country or the world in general if we never saw eye to eye on any issue? What would be the consequences of being for something, and then when we find out the opposing side supports it, we turn vehemently against it? What happens when we agree on where to go and even what cocktails we're going to have when we get there, but because of wrangling, partisanship, prejudice, ingrained beliefs or just out of pure ass-hole-ness we never get started?

Is the divide between us really as big as it seems? The canyon that is portrayed by the media for dramatic effect seems to work on a lot of us. If we don't think about it, it would appear there is actually a canyon between us. The portrayal is part of the problem; but the root of the matter is we must think about what we are being told, instead of just blindly inhaling it. We must strive towards the middle where we all can meet, not the outer edges where we can all fall off a cliff.

It's easier to see eye to eye when we see and ponder what the truth actually is. It's not about what makes us different, but what makes us the same.

I MUST CONSTANTLY REINFORCE THIS AS A MADMAN FOR GOOD!!!!

ENTRY #101

1/26/12 - 4:04pm

ANOTHER MANIFESTO OF A MADMAN FOR GOOD

Do we always want things we can't have or things we can't imagine are possible? Do we pine and worry over things we have control over and do nothing about, or things we have control over and do everything under the sun about? Is seeing or concentrating on what we don't have an enriching and useful tool that motivates us to bigger and better things? Or does concentrating on what we don't have and not concentrating on what we do have prevent us from achieving our goals?

Maybe we should stop and think what's important to us and then start our action plan from there. We should make a priority list so we know what the best use of our time is. Maybe we just need to be present, and stop and think about what's actually transpiring all around us.

Sometimes we think about what's best for us, and sometime we think about what's worse for us; that's the game of life, a constant struggle for our enlightenment. We simply must remember that we need to be happy about what we have, have it fill us up, and then strive for more. Imagination is what makes life interesting. We must fill up our own cup, so we can fill up others.

THIS IS ONE OF MY REALIZATIONS AS A MADMAN FOR GOOD!!!!

ENTRY# 102

1/26/12 - 4:17pm

ANOTHER MANIFESTO OF MADMAN FOR GOOD

Once we fill our own cup with happy moments and the joy that warms our soul, then what? Do we spread it to others so they can feel it also? Do we keep it for ourselves so we can continue to enrich our own being, forgetting about everybody else because they have their own problems? Do we waste happy moments by hoarding them and not spreading them for fear that they would lose their purpose? Or is the very reason we make ourselves happy and take care of our souls is so we can show others they can feel self-love like we do?

We can all come to a place where balance can be achieved, where we do for ourselves and do for others, where we don't have to choose between the two. Maybe this is what keeps life fresh and in good working order. Maybe we need to realize balance exists before we can harness it, because once we do, what we are supposed to do next will appear to us. Maybe it's on the other side of that door and we just have to walk through it.

I MUST STAY CONSCIOUS OF THIS AS A MADMAN FOR GOOD!!!!

ENTRY #103

1/26/12 – 4:27pm

ANOTHER MANIFESTO OF A MADMAN FOR GOOD

Is the reason we tear each other down and degrade one another the same reason we didn't want to be picked last for the team when we were in grade school? Is it because we feel an uncontrollable need to be accepted into the pack so we won't be seen as an enemy or a threat? Do we want to be accepted so others will recognize our efforts and build us up into their pre-fab image of us? Or do we tear others down because we don't like them and perceive them as having wronged us, so we just want them to suffer?

We need to look at the root of all problems however hard or complex they may be so we can acknowledge them, attempt to help or heal them, and then let them go. We have an uncanny dependence on what our peers comment about when a discussion comes up. Maybe we need to try the opposite of how we have been trying to solve problems. We should try building each other up instead of tearing each other down and see if where we end up isn't exactly where we dreamt of being. Everything happens in life for a reason, and the question of whether we will evolve might come down to how we treat others.

I MUST FIGURE THIS OUT AS A MADMAN FOR GOOD!!!!

ENTRY# 104

1/26/12 – 4:38pm

ANOTHER MANIFESTO OF A MADMAN FOR GOOD

Does the main office of leadership deserve to be respected in any country, even if a person's rival party is holding that office? Do talkers and pundits drone on endlessly about what's right to say to a President and what's not okay? Do the pundits actually mean what they say, or are they just saying it to get a rise out of people, to boost their ratings and to collect a hefty paycheck? Is respect gained or earned? When a person is in a position of power and authority, should the office itself be respected more than the actual person holding that office? Is this a no brainer, or is it going to take some deep thought?

Maybe when a voter gets their party elected, they expect a certain amount of professional courtesy they may or may not be entitled to, and maybe the opposite happens when an opposing party gets elected.

Maybe it's the root problem that's causing all our hurt and mistrust on the surface. Maybe our disrespect for each other is emanating from ignorance ingrained in us over generations; if this is true, we have major problems. Republicans tear down Democrats, and vice versa; but when dog whistles and coded language are used, respect isn't even a blip on the radar.

I MUST KEEP ASKING THIS AS A MADMAN FOR GOOD!!!!

ENTRY #105

1/26/12 – 4:51pm

ANOTHER MANIFESTO OF MADMAN FOR GOOD

Does the disrespect we deal with (and sometimes create) in our daily lives translate to the vitriol we see in the political arena? Is what we act on, what we say and what we think directly correlated to candidates or existing elected officials tearing each other to shreds? Do we have influence over them, or do they have an influence over us? Do we have a choice? The Rolling Stones singing Sympathy for the Devil said it best, "I shouted out who killed the Kennedys, but after all, it was you and me." Does that mean we were literally the assailant or assailants that shot Kennedy? Or does it mean that we created the evil ideas, prejudices and hysteria that created a person like Oswald or the shooting to even happen in the first place?

Maybe we will see over time that our thoughts and actions have a ripple effect that spread out further than our eyes can see. Maybe we don't see what we do affects others, maybe we don't care. Maybe there will come a day when those of us who don't care will become rare, obsolete and found nowhere in the mainstream; which will only happen if we see the ripple effects we create, how what we say can hurt others and how it can drive them mad. Will we be ready with pitchfork and torch or olive branch in hand?

I MUST CONSTANTLY STAY AWARE OF THIS AS A MADMAN FOR GOOD!!!!

ENTRY #106

1/28/12 – 4:11pm

ANOTHER MANIFESTO OF A MADMAN FOR GOOD

We've all been through the loss of something we were positive would be there forever, what does it mean? Maybe we don't completely lose the thing, maybe its form changes from its original shape thereby changing its inherent meaning, but what then? Maybe the loss hasn't happened yet; can we stop it, do we have the power?

Life is constantly changing its form to keep us on our toes and making sure we're paying attention to what's really important. It's as though events are happening completely at random, but are they? Maybe it's because life is random, mixed with our free will and ability to make choices, that allows us to rise to an understanding that we never thought possible.

As we go through life, we will have gains and losses, positive and negative, yin and yang. The greatest thing we can do for ourselves and the planet is pay attention, be conscious and don't take everything at face value, especially all at the same time.

THIS IS SOMETHING I AM CONSTANTLY LEARNING AS A MADMAN FOR GOOD!!!!

ENTRY# 107

1/28/12 – 4:27pm

ANOTHER MANIFESTO OF A MADMAN FOR GOOD

If everything is random yet we exercise free will and choice at the same time, how do we prepare for life? If we are told to expect the unexpected, but at the same time know our experiences can shape unexpected events, is it even possible to draw up a plan? If every story has 2 sides, 3 sides or 84 sides with a truth mixed in that is perceived differently by all who observe it, what drives us?

Life is a constant challenge whose possibilities grow when our understanding and consciousness grows. Once we have a greater understanding of the whys and how's, we might be able to figure out what's been holding back our collective evolution for the past few thousand years.

I MUST WORK TOWARD THIS AS A MADMAN FOR GOOD!!!!

ENTRY #108

1/28/12 – 4:35pm

ANOTHER MANIFESTO OF A MADMAN FOR GOOD

Once we raise our overall understanding and realize that most of us go through many of the same challenges, we will have given ourselves the ability to change our destiny; maybe we have always had this ability, it just might have taken the right moment to flip the switch within our souls.

It is possible for us to get to a place where we aren't in gridlock with every political solution we can think up. It is possible for partisan divides to melt away and be shown as the fake, destructive and distractive force they really are. It is possible for us to treat everybody how we would like to be treated. It is possible to end discrimination, racism, sexism and militarism in our generation, in our time, right now.

All these things are possible; if there are forces out there that say they aren't, they're just trying to prove their point. Why don't we try to prove ours?

I MUST INSIST ON THIS AS A MADMAN FOR GOOD!!!!

ENTRY# 109

1/28/12 – 4:46pm

ANOTHER MANIFESTO OF A MADMAN FOR GOOD

Is there a universal formula for creating a perfect and unrelenting utopian society? Is there a way a plan could actually be drawn up that we could all agree on? Is it possible that everything were thinking now, everything we thought about in the past, or will think about in the future will always be the right and true thing? Is there a value system that all seven billion people on this planet could abide by? Is there a religion that is the only true vehicle to the enlightenment we all seek? Is there a way everyone should conduct themselves, who they should marry or who they should love? Is it possible we're all the same?

No, none of this is possible.

I MUST DRIVE THIS POINT HOME AS A MADMAN FOR GOOD!!!!

ENTRY #110

1/28/12 – 4:55pm

ANOTHER MANIFESTO OF A MADMAN FOR GOOD

It's important we figure out what is possible and what isn't so we can sift through all the possibilities in life, but is that the end point? Does the universal goal of humankind have the same end game, or does the sheer fact that there could be a universal goal point out the hypocrisy in propaganda, which is part of the reason we get distracted from what's really important in the first place? Or is it possible that our goals are the same but different at the same time?

Maybe we will float through life overwhelmed by the vast volume and density of the root issues plaguing our species. Maybe we will stampede through life, not letting anything get in our way because we are so sure of our path and its righteousness. Or maybe we float, then we sink, then we rise to that perfect, level flying that all of us strive for.

I MUST WORK TO FIND THIS OUT AS A MADMAN FOR GOOD!!!!

ENTRY #111

1/30/12 – 7:53am

ANOTHER MANIFESTO OF A MADMAN FOR GOOD

If there are evil corporations, evil bureaucracies, evil presidents, evil prime ministers and/or evil actions taken by all, how do we counteract them? When we get bombarded with negative messages and images on a daily basis, how do we balance it out with good and positive messages? When all is dark, how do we make the light peek through?

Life presents many challenges and tests what kind of character or person we think we are. If we are loyal to a certain company and love their products, would we be able to boycott them if they commit a heinous act or if an endemic predatory policy is revealed? If we build up a positive image in our head of a president or other head of state, then that person is caught embezzling, stealing babies, murdering for their own needs and not the country they represent, or even if we found out our favorite president is a liar, how would we process it?

If there is anything we need to remember on this crazy journey called life, it is the possibility our psyche will be tested at every opportunity. We must be honest and true to ourselves, so we can be honest and true to others.

I MUST CULTIVATE THIS AS A MADMAN FOR GOOD!!!!

ENTRY #112

1/30/12 – 8:07pm

ANOTHER MANIFESTO OF A MADMAN FOR GOOD

If our character, psyche and demeanor will be tested at expectedly unexpected times, is there a way to be ready for it? Is there a method for all of us to just get along, coexist and live side by side without killing one another? Will we be able to stop judging each other (even subconsciously) so we can get at the heart and root of an issue and who someone really is? Are we able to say I like this person for this reason, and I don't like that person for that reason without judging who we're talking about?

Once we open ourselves up to all of life's possibilities, we are open to everything, positive and negative. We must be vigilant in our pursuits of the truth, but humble enough to admit when we're wrong and might have prejudged a situation. We aren't perfect; we will not succeed all the time 24-7 & 365. But, if we use our love for humankind as our guide in life, we will travel in the right direction.

THIS IS ONE OF THE THINGS I HAVE TO FIGURE OUT AS A MADMAN FOR GOOD!!!!

ENTRY #113

1/30/12 – 8:19am

ANOTHER MANIFESTO OF A MADMAN FOR GOOD

When an average person, candidate for office, an office holder themselves, group or other entity commits fraud, is there a universal way of dealing with them?

If the average person steals, insider trades or covers up a grand criminal scheme, do or should they get treated the same as a business leader or politician, whether or not that person presently holds a position of power? Is this a conflict of interest? Is this called "I have more power and influence than you because of my office or position, therefore I am above the law?" Or does it really mean with great power and influence comes great responsibility and great accountability?

 There are many politicians, heads of state, diplomats, CEOS and private contractors that think they're above the law and therefore not accountable to anybody; people like you and me who might not have power and influence always seem to get whatever crumbs they decide to leave us.

It is imperative whenever we get sad or depressed because of the statement above for us to remember that powerful people are actually more accountable than the rest of us because of their position; their misdeeds can be covered up on a much bigger scale, but they can also be exposed on a much grander scale as well. We all must do the exposing.

I MUST DRIVE THIS POINT HOME AS A MADMAN FOR GOOD!!!!

ENTRY #114

1/30/12 – 8:35am

ANOTHER MANIFESTO OF A MADMAN FOR GOOD

If people in positions of power are more powerful than the rest of us, but more accountable at the same time, is it because critical mass can ebb any tide? If we got enough angry people together to voice our frustrations and carry out authentic actions that could help right the ship for everyone, could or would the powerful do the same? Could they amass the same monstrous sized group to demand redress of their grievances?

Would the "powerbrokers" get people to come out who believed their passion and belief of an issue was at stake, or would they have to pay participants to be there because critical mass on either side of an issue is really part of the same gelatinous blob?

The "non-elites" can gather people because of their passions, beliefs and convictions mostly because they don't have power and influence. When the "elites" want to counteract this perceived insurrection by establishing their own critical mass, they find it much harder to locate people willing to struggle when they already have money and power; this is because they only care to fight when it's about gaining more money and power.

The only way the "elites" could keep up with the non-elite's numbers in critical mass situations, is through conversion and/or coercion. We must be eternally vigilant so we never get transitioned to a place where we are forced to hold or support a platform that goes completely against our own needs.

THIS IS ONE OF THE THINGS I MUST PUSH FOR AS A MADMAN FOR GOOD!!!!

ENTRY #115

1/30/12 – 8:48am

ANOTHER MANIFESTO OF A MADMAN FOR GOOD

How do we avoid getting lured, persuaded or transitioned to something that goes completely against everything we stand for, and goes completely against our needs? How can we live out the inherent authenticity that makes up each and every one of our souls? How can we be more real, honest and down to earth people who realize what's really important?

Maybe we could start each day by being thankful for our life, and then doing something nurturing for ourselves. Maybe we could start a project we've been putting off, continue a project we already started; or just be content that we woke up and are breathing. To avoid letting bad energy lure us from the path we know is true, we have to be confident in the person we are and the person we'd like to be.

Powerful entities are able to lure weak entities because they see all the misdirection and confusion bouncing around, they offer some direction and provide a path. Let's show the powerful that we don't need their path, we already have our own.

I MUST BUILD THIS UP AS A MADMAN FOR GOOD!!!!

ENTRY #116

1/31/12 – 7:34am

ANOTHER MANIFESTO OF A MADMAN FOR GOOD

Is there a different way of electing a president other than allowing unlimited money to "indirectly" flow to the candidates? Is there a way to hold an election without having a billion dollars flow to any one single candidate?

Is it possible there are forces that have been cultivating and growing this outcome for years which are only now starting to bear fruit? Could or will it take just as long for the tides to flow back the other way?

Some of us misrepresent the invaluable tool of free speech to say that corporations are people and that money is speech. Maybe in this view corporations are like the rest of us, and money is just like free speech, therefore contributing unlimited money is just exercising free speech rights.

What if some of us start to uncover all the lies and deceit that this method of election produces and how the problem goes much deeper towards insider trading, tax shelters and more, will the rest of us stand up against it?

Some of us might say that corporations are people with free speech rights, but we all should know that a group of people that make up a corporation don't add up to one person with one voice.

Flesh and blood people are entities that breathe, have hearts, and know the fight ahead will be thick with fog.

THIS IS ONE OF THE MYTHS I MUST FIGHT TO DISPELL WITH OVERT, OBVIOUS AND EASILY EXPLAINABLE DETAILED FACT AS A MADMAN FOR GOOD!!!!

ENTRY #117

1/31/12 – 7:47am

ANOTHER MANIFESTO OF A MADMAN FOR GOOD

If we are at a point in our collective evolution where entities made up of many people are considered one person, what's to stop that "one" person with all their concentrated power from taking over governmental functions? What's to stop this "one" person from getting drunk with power, and destroying anything and everything that blocks their path from the domination they seek? What if a group of people who don't work for a company, yet speak with one voice as useful members of a coalition fighting to counteract current trends, then what?

If Citizens United is allowed to stand and people just keep getting more powerful and more influential in our elections, what will they look like in 20 years? If our voting is already like a three ring circus with all the gaffes and mud being slung, how will it look when one company is running against another company for who will run the country? Is it possible we could have Gatorade running against IBM in the 2032 elections? Does this all sound crazy? If we as flesh and blood humans don't do something and stand up to stop the tsunami of money in politics, that is exactly what we will get, and it only gets worse from there.

I MUST REMIND MYSELF OF THIS AS WELL AS OTHERS AS I BECOME A MADMAN FOR GOOD!!!!

ENTRY# 118

1/31/12 – 7:59am

ANOTHER MANIFESTO OF A MADMAN FOR GOOD

If a candidate attacks another candidate when both are running for the same office, does it discourage votes for their opponent? Do candidates use attacks to distract the voting public from analyzing them and their record they would rather keep in a locked closet? Is the problem that candidates feel inadequate to their peers, so they tear down their opponents as a way of building themselves up? Or is it to play to the ignorance of the populace when they only talk about what the other guy doesn't do so they never have to talk about what they do?

Maybe candidates for office want to keep their skeletons in the closet where no voter, reporter or internal affairs investigator can ever find them. Maybe they pull the wool over our eyes and say they want to create jobs and lower taxes for everybody, when all they really want is jobs and low or non-existent taxes for themselves and their inner circle. The answer lies in the fact that when candidates badger each other, it feels like real life to some of us, because we might badger people in our own lives. Maybe for candidates to speak with purpose for the people and about "real issues", we as a people need to start a humanistic conversation, so candidates not only start playing to it, but start believing it as well.

THIS ONE OF THE TIDES I MUST TURN AS A MADMAN FOR GOOD!!!!

ENTRY #119

1/31/12 – 8:12am

ANOTHER MANIFESTO OF A MADMAN FOR GOOD

Does it take a genius to figure out what all of us want as a people? Does it take a rocket scientist to decipher the chaos that is daily life and human evolution? Does Steven Hawking himself have to literally come through our door and break down in layman's terms the ins and outs of quantum physics and thermodynamics for us to figure out why we do the things we do?

It is true that we are all unique as individuals, but very similar at the same time. We all want a good economy that is fair to all and provides a decent living for us, especially if we want to start a family, or continue to support one. We all want companies and businesses to pay a decent wage we could all live off of. We all want a good education so we know why a problem happens by looking at its root source. We all want to be remembered, we all want to matter.

Are we really that different than one another; are we really that hard to figure out? Maybe we need to look in the mirror, and then side to side.

I MUST DRIVE THIS POINT HOME AS A MADMAN FOR GOOD!!!!

ENTRY #120

1/31/12 – 8:22am

ANOTHER MANIFESTO OF A MADMAN FOR GOOD

When we wake up in the morning, what is the first thought that pops into our heads? Is it about work, family, the kids, the bills, the house or how crappy our life might be? Is it something we might not have control over? Is it the thought that from the moment we step out of bed, it's all downhill from there? Or is it about how beautiful a day it is, and that were thankful to be alive?

When we roll out of bed, or sometimes before we roll out, we should think about all the good we can accomplish if we really concentrate on it; we would feel adequate to the task and be willing to go out there and grab the day by the short hairs. We should never let ourselves feel inferior to our peers, and know that whatever actions we take will only cause others to drive this point home.

If we awoke every day and said thank you, (we might just have to think it and not even to say it) how would our day turnout? The idea of being thankful for who we are and what we have, so it motivates us to accomplish or receive what we don't have, is what makes the day worth getting out of bed. It is how we should start our day, by filling our own cup, and then we have plenty to give to others.

I MUST REMEMBER THIS FOR OTHERS AND ESPECIALLY FOR MYSELF AS A MADMAN FOR GOOD!!!!

ENTRY #121

2/1/12 – 7:45am

ANOTHER MANIFESTO OF A MADMAN FOR GOOD

What is happening to the news media when an admitted satirist and comedian gives more in-depth information about a news story in five minutes, than a 24 hours cable news channel can in two hours? Does this discrepancy happen because the 24-7 stations are on all day, so they have to put some kind of story out there even though it might not be fully investigated or might be pure speculation? Is it because comedians are taking observational humor and making it relevant and biting by throwing pieces of truth in? Are news people that are caught up in producing infotainment and not information moving closer to being comedians? Are comedians in being more astute in looking at societal problems, moving closer to the people? When by the way was it okay for reporters to release speculation, have round table discussions involving host experts, governmental and business leaders and call it news?

When a lot of us get our news from comedians instead of reporters, where does is it lead? Maybe all this stems from people just trying to get ratings or a few laughs. Now if comedians and news people could get both laughs and ratings, while informing the public and making them think critically at the same time, we would all be a lot better off.

ANOTHER THING I MUST HELP TO BRING ON AS A MADMAN FOR GOOD!!!!

ENTRY #122

2/1/12 – 7:59am

ANOTHER MANIFESTO OF A MADMAN FOR GOOD

If comedians are attempting to be more like news people, and news people are attempting to more like comedians, what will the situation look like in 20 years? Will we have CNN anchors moonlighting on Comedy Central and HBO with their new special? Will we have standup comedians and funny TV actors highlighting on CNN, MSNBC and FOX NEWS? Will there just be no news available for those of us who can't figure out the subtleties of a certain joke? Or will all of it devolve into some kind of gelatinous amalgamation of items and people we used to know, but now are completely unrecognizable to us? Maybe we should take a news story or joke we see or hear and ask ourselves this, is there any truth in it, and if there is, how can we help others to see and hear it as well?

With the closing of many foreign bureaus and investigative units in the mainstream media, and the 24-7 news and infotainment cycle taking its place, it's not hard to figure out what the media has devolved into; big corporate buyouts that have caused massive consolidation. Given all that, we need information because we like to know what's happening around us. As long as we think critically about the information we get whether it be from a comedian or newsie, we will be able to make informed thoughts.

I MUST DECIPHER THIS MORE AS A MADMAN FOR GOOD!!!!

ENTRY #123

2/1/12 – 8:11am

ANOTHER MANIFESTO OF A MADMAN FOR GOOD

Distractions are all around us and come from all directions; some come in the form of pictures, movies or even books that we greatly enjoy, but still keep us from what we were planning. Some distractions are friends or family members asking us to go to dinner, the beach, a movie, or just outside somewhere we know we would enjoy, but still prevent us from doing what we planned. Some distractions come from news outlets, talking heads, and what used to be reporters, government and business leaders who are trying to not only add to their bottom lines, but also distract us because they don't want us to know what's really going on and what they're really planning. They figure if we keep fighting amongst ourselves and buying materialistic crap we don't need, we will be pacified, won't see what's really going on, and therefore wouldn't unite and rise up to stop the whole damn thing.

Knowing the distractions are out there is the first step. The second step is to decipher the distractions and their root and truthful definitions so we can slow and then end their sinister intentions.

I MUST VIGILANTLY INVESTIGATE THIS AS A MADMAN FOR GOOD!!!!

ENTRY #124

2/1/12 – 8:23am

ANOTHER MANIFESTO OF A MADMAN FOR GOOD

Once we are able to pick and choose what's real and what's not out of all the information that bombards us daily, and figure out what distractions exist and what they mean, can we just shout it from the rooftops so everybody can hear? Would it sound like gibberish because we haven't put in enough time studying the distractions and deciphering what the root B.S. is, or would it sound like that line from the 70s movie The Network, "I'm as mad as hell, and I can't take it anymore?"

If we find a method that works for us in making sense out of the thick fog of news and distractions, will that same method work for others? If our understanding comes from hearing a certain truth, would simply telling somebody else about that truth be enough to reach them as well? Or would it end up like that movie The Network again; where the journalist sees the truth, tells his audience about his anger and how they should be angry too, and then gets discredited because he divulged information that was so real and true that it turned people's worlds upside down, and they stopped believing him. Shouting from the rooftops is good and can work, as long as we realize some of us are at different places in the evolution of our understanding.

I HAVE TO REMEMBER THIS WHEN I ESPOUSE INFORMATION AS A MADMAN FOR GOOD!!!!

ENTRY #125

2/1/12 – 8:36am

ANOTHER MANIFESTO OF A MADMAN FOR GOOD

It's kind of funny how we end up in the same place time and time again, historical event after historical event and still make some of the same mistakes we made a thousand years ago. Like the old saying, "if we don't learn from history were doomed to repeat it", I would take it a step further and say if we don't learn from the past and help each other learn the lessons of the present, there will be a much bleaker future than any of us could imagine. It is a little comical and I chuckle when I hear a politician talk about some new idea or platform that will revolutionize or galvanize the people and take them into the wild blue yonder, when you could witness candidates and elected officials on any given day saying the same exact thing 40 years ago.

We must learn from where we went wrong, but also from where we went right. If we can only prove our way will work if we don't think critically about it, a populace of ignorant and dumb people will emerge. If our ideas are only provable in theory because when attempted they fail miserably, it might behoove us to look for real world solutions to real world problems; the key is being a member of the real world.

I MUST REMEMBER TO THINK ABOUT WHAT IM CHUCKLING OVER AND WHY AS A MADMAN FOR GOOD!!!!

ENTRY# 126

2/2/12 – 4:11pm

ANOTHER MANIFESTO OF A MADMAN FOR GOOD

When somebody says they don't care or aren't concerned with the very poor or the very rich because they feel both groups are "covered", are they lying, or did they let their personal truth slip out? Is it different if a candidate for office says they're opposed to a certain person or group of people than if a civilian did because it's a way for them to get elected by or supported by a certain group? Does it make it any less despicable? Do we not take a civilian as seriously because they don't or won't soon have the power and influence of elected office?

Maybe somebody running for office is trying to appeal to a certain segment of the population because they feel it's their path to being elected. Maybe a civilian is trying to fit in with a certain group of friends, and thinks that if they disparage the very poor they'll be accepted into an inner circle. Maybe since elected officials or candidates were civilians at one point, they are just repeating what's worked for them before. Maybe civilians should step into the shoes of the poor so they don't evolve into overzealous and egotistical politicians.

THIS IS SOMETHING I NEED TO INTRODUCE AS A MADMAN FOR GOOD!!!!

ENTRY #127

2/2/12 – 4:24pm

ANOTHER MANIFESTO OF A MADMAN FOR GOOD

If privileged civilians become privileged candidates who become privileged office holders, what if any reason would they have for not caring about their privileged friends? If we are born with a lot of money, run for office, get elected and make a lot more money, what reason would we have to not keep the gravy train rolling along? If we make a lot of money because of our own talent, would it be different than somebody who was always rich? Is old money really any different than new money? Are there people out there who believe money is the path to prosperity and not the root of all evil?

Sometimes privilege is handed down and sometimes it's earned. Sometimes rich people like to throw their money in people's faces and sometimes they like to keep it to themselves; sometimes they even donate to charity. Sometimes the rich are actually good hearted people that use their wealth and privilege to help heal the planet.

Rich people that don't care about the poor need to be shown that their actions are hurtful, and have consequences; even for themselves!

I MUST DECIPHER THIS AS A MADMAN FOR GOOD!!!!

ENTRY #128

2/2/12 – 4:35pm

ANOTHER MANIFESTO OF A MADMAN FOR GOOD

Once we establish that other people (including people in power) have the same human needs as ourselves and will prosper immensely through transparency and accountability, what concrete steps can we take in our daily lives to make it happen? What can we do on a daily basis that can help us contribute to the positive evolution of the human race? What can we work into our schedule? How can we reorganize our priorities so as to shed light on our highest good? How can we be better citizens of earth and humanity?

I would love to say I have the blanket, black and white and all-encompassing answer of what we should do that would solve all the problems for everybody on earth, but I don't. The fact that we know the bigger ideas and questions are out there, and are trying to incorporate them into our daily lives, lets us rest comfortably knowing we've taken the first and second steps in our own personal and unique journey, where will it lead to next?

I MUST ALWAYS ASSESS THIS AS A MADMAN FOR GOOD!!!!

ENTRY #129

2/2/12 – 4:45pm

ANOTHER MANIFESTO OF A MADMAN FOR GOOD

When racism, darkness and evil permeate our government, (and therefore our people) how do we show it for the terrible and ignorant hoax that it is? How should we respond if we are attacked personally? Would it be different for us if we found out somebody else had been attacked? Would it make any difference if the attack was physical or verbal? Should we go at the problem full bore every time wherever and whenever it happens? Should we wait and strategize the best way to end it? Or should we investigate, uncover and dispel the root of it all, therefore stopping it from happening in the first place?

We can't possibly know every time racism or darkness will rear its ugly head, but we can prepare for how we're going to handle it. Should we just yell, swear and demean other people until they cower in the corner, crying like little babies? Do we turn the other cheek and walk away, therefore breaking the cycle of viciousness? Or do we take everything on a case by case basis?

Everybody has heard the old line that talk is cheap, well it is; but sometimes the price rises so fast and so high that we must fight, or must consciously walk away.

I MUST CONSTANTLY REMIND MYSELF OF THIS AS A MADMAN FOR GOOD!!!!

ENTRY# 130

2/2/12 – 4:58pm

ANOTHER MANIFESTO OF A MADMAN FOR GOOD

If the fight ahead for justice is going to be as long and hard as we expect it to be, what is the motivation for us to keep going? When the days are dark and it looks like everything is going downhill extremely fast, how do we tell ourselves there is a brighter future out there? How do we get psyched about getting involved in the fight, how do we know we'll make it through? How do we strive for the light at the end of the tunnel?

The key is to find what our passion or passions are so we can be more focused on our goals. Maybe we need to evaluate the pros and cons of getting involved in a conflict. Maybe all we need to remember is that there are a lot of people out there way worse off than us that would love to have the problem of figuring out what their passion is.

We need to remember the question why, should we get involved or shouldn't we? At the end of the day, the only thing that keeps us motivated and striving for that collective "better" day, is never forgetting why we are here and why others need our help. We need to be aware of others plights and what stirs our passions, because it will give us the motivation we need to keep going.

I MUST CONSTANTLY RE-AFFIRM THIS WITHIN MYSELF AS A MADMAN FOR GOOD!!!!

ENTRY #131

2/3/12 – 4:14pm

ANOTHER MANIFESTO OF A MADMAN FOR GOOD

If we all grow consciously to the point of getting past distractions and our differences (and it is a big "if" because we have choice and free will) it will have been because we worked together to fight all injustice, corporate greed, and unfair taxes. We must fight against war and stand for peace, so we can achieve a humanistic acceptance of all cultures, society and way of life. How can we integrate all this into our daily lives and ingrained routines?

We all must start with being thankful for what we have at the beginning of each and every day, because there is always somebody out there that has it way worse. Once we realize there are people out there who have it worse than us, we can work on being thankful from that point forward. When we are thankful, it fills us up with the loving authentic confidence that requires action to undertake important tasks in front of us. We can and we must always remember what's truly important and worth our time and energy.

I MUST USE THIS AS A STARTING POINT AS A MADMAN FOR GOOD!!!!

ENTRY #132

2/3/12 – 4:25pm

ANOTHER MANIFESTO OF A MADMAN FOR GOOD

How can we grow conscious one might ask? What steps will imprint an exact blueprint in our minds of what we can and must do to take on the struggle for our soul? Is there a way for it not to be a struggle, but an understanding?

We must look inside ourselves to find out what drives us; it might be a huge challenge for some of us, but the end results will more than make up for all the hard work put in. When we start the day being thankful, we must make it a point to smile at somebody we don't know. Try it, walk up to somebody or near them and just smile, see what they do. Will they smile back, who knows? The point is spreading a good thought to people we come into contact with, (even if we don't know them) so they spread it to people they come into contact with, and so on, is what makes the world go round. Some might call it, "paying it forward", I call it what we must do to survive.

I know smiling might seem like an easy or cheesy example, but if we can't even be human enough to smile at one another, we have a very long road to travel to get where we want to go.

I MUST REMEMBER WE ALL GOT TO START SOMEWHERE AS I EMBARK AS A MADMAN FOR GOOD!!!!

ENTRY #133

2/3/12 – 4:38pm

ANOTHER MANIFESTO OF A MADMAN FOR GOOD

If we smile and are civil as we pass each other during the day, will we then see each other as human when we start talking? Can we authentically make an effort towards striking up a conversation with somebody? Will we have the strength to carry on if our plans don't work out the way we want the first time, or ever? Do we have the strength to know that, "I am my brother's keeper" is really a way of life that permeates all our interactions? Is it going to happen soon, or might it take a while?

If we are able to start the conversation and begin talking to each other, we can convince ourselves that people are just people. If we realize that we're all human when we communicate, we will begin to realize the full breadth of its implications, and we will see how we can come together like we haven't in the past.

Maybe it would make all the tough questions a little easier to answer if we just slow down and simply listen to the root of the problem.

I MUST TRY THIS AS A MADMAN FOR GOOD!!!!

ENTRY #134

2/3/12 – 4:50pm

ANOTHER MANIFESTO OF A MADMAN FOR GOOD

A "dreamer" once said that if we don't know what to do or we don't know how to act, that with trials comes understanding, and with understanding appears a world where we can see each other in ourselves. When we are able to relate to one another, we can begin to solve problems because personal attacks will be nothing but an afterthought; this afterthought is the last hurdle we must clear before the real work can begin.

We must see and live in a time when all of us can live and be so all of us can live and be. Maybe there will be challenges and tests we must face in order to be worthy of this prize; I only say prize because it will make us think we're winning something, which will keep us interested if we feel like running away from a terribly materialistic and phony world. Maybe we can achieve greatness.

I think those of us who are there willing to start, must now start. Those needing more time, take the time, but be conscious of why you are.

I MUST REALIZE WE ARE ALL DREAMERS AND CREATORS AS I MAKE THIS ATTEMPT AS A MADMAN FOR GOOD!!!!

ENTRY #135

2/3/12 – 5:01pm

ANOTHER MANIFESTO OF A MADMAN FOR GOOD

Have we ever been out somewhere where it's all peaceful and a beautiful day, the birds are chirping, the sun is out, it's warm, but somebody's damn car alarm starts blaring? Have we ever been cruising through a beautiful and glorious day and a screechingly loud noise starts blaring in our ears? Do we tune it out? Are we able to just go about our time like it's not even there? Do we stop what we're doing and listen? Or do we wait for the alarm to stop, or wonder why it's going off in the first place? Do we listen, or not?

When we get tired of the same old routine, we should ask ourselves why? Maybe we should start asking, "Hey, does anybody know why this car alarm is going off?" Maybe we even walk over to the car to see if somebody is in the process of breaking into it, maybe we are the only one that hears it. Maybe it was meant for us to stop, take notice, and then reassess our own situation.

We might get interruptions wherever we go, whether we pay attention to them or not depends on whether we are ready to receive the information or not.

I MUST BE RELENTLESSLY AWARE AS A MADMAN FOR GOOD!!!!

ENTRY# 136

2/5/12 – 8:12am

ANOTHER MANIFESTO OF A MADMAN FOR GOOD

If we only have one shot on this earth, (or many depending on what we believe in or what lessons we might have yet to learn) how are we going to treat people along the way while we are achieving our goals? If we don't think about anybody but ourselves, and not see who or what we might be stepping on or in on our way to the top, what will we have really achieved? If we treat each other well, are there for each other when we need a helping hand and act solely from the thankfulness we feel in our soul that lovingly spews forth, will we achieve more than if we were unthankful and uncaring jerks? Will we enjoy life more if we're good from the start, because we remember good things happen to good people and our goals will be achieved if we are just good people?

There definitely comes a time in all of our lives when we begin to ask ourselves about the meaning of life and where we are going. Then the question might come up about how the journey to get there might be achieved smoothly with no bumps or dips. Acting like a good person isn't the same as being a good person. We have to really feel it within ourselves, so everybody else can feel it within themselves.

I MUST NEVER FORGET THIS AS A MADMAN FOR GOOD!!!!

ENTRY #137

2/5/12 – 8:24am

ANOTHER MANIFESTO OF A MADMAN FOR GOOD

If we're good people, and we interact with caring and kindness toward everybody we come into contact with, (even the ones that aren't caring and kind to us) will there be a time when it all comes together?

When some people say what we need is more than just love, and simply being a good person will lead us into destitution and eventual unhappiness, are they actually looking at what love can do? Are they thinking about what causes us to be good people and what actions and events will just naturally come to us?

What or where being a good person will lead us is unknown, but one thing is certain, we have to find our journey's real purpose. If we say being a good person just isn't enough, we should ask ourselves why we think that. Do we picture the bum on the street with a smile that waves to everybody that goes by as a good person?

Is the young man who helps an old lady across the street a good person? What about the person who works 50 to 60 hours a week to support their family, are they a good person?

We go through our entire life trying to figure out what a good person is and what actions we should take in a given situation.

We must never forget that being a good person and having love in our hearts can take many forms. We can rely on the fact that living is much easier and better when we aren't jerks.

I MUST HAVE THIS IMPRINTED ON MY BRAIN AS A MADMAN FOR GOOD!!!!

ENTRY #138

2/5/12 – 8:38am

ANOTHER MANIFESTO OF A MADMAN FOR GOOD

There is an old saying that goes; "the only sure thing in life is death and taxes, and close only counts in horse shoes and hand grenades," is it true? Is there a way in this amazingly complex life we step out into every day that we can say something is going to go down, it's a guarantee? With so many actions, events, people and countless variables flying at us the second we walk out the door, how can we know any of them will be a sure thing? How do we know it will lead us to prosperity and not to ruin?

Doesn't the very notion of going out and expecting the unexpected, (which by definition is not known to us) prove that we can't possibly know for sure what will happen? Can the idea ever be general and/or across the board? Is it different for everybody because all of us are unique, but operate on the same basic premise?

We must figure out for ourselves what we feel is real and guaranteed, because it will be different than what our neighbor feels. Similarities happen when we realize we all go through the same processes.

I MUST COMFORT MYSELF WITH THIS AS A MADMAN FOR GOOD!!!!

ENTRY #139

2/5/12 – 8:51am

ANOTHER MANIFESTO OF A MADMAN FOR GOOD

Is it a possibility that with all the uncertainty, hardships and challenges we experience, they are just tests? Have we ever been going along and one thing after another happens that we can't explain? What does expecting the unexpected really mean? Does it mean going through life not knowing where to go or what to do so the only comfortable option is to curl up in the fetal position? Or does it mean being humble, not acting like or thinking we know everything and realizing that things will happen sometimes that are beyond our control?

If we are being tested, by whom or what is the purpose?

Building our character and actively seeking out what's best for us and the planet can only happen when we are true to ourselves. If we are good people, interacting out of purely good intentions, whatever test or challenge comes up, we will be ready. Even though it's unexpected, the love we take will only be equal to the love we make.

I MUST REMEMBER EVERYBODY GOES THROUGH DIFFERENT TESTS AS I JOURNEY AS A MADMAN FOR GOOD!!!!

ENTRY # 140

2/5/12 – 9:03am

ANOTHER MANIFESTO OF A MADMAN FOR GOOD

Have we ever been in a rush because everything doesn't seem to be happening fast enough? Has there been a time when we begin to grow tired from all the blood, sweat and tears we have poured into something, and it hasn't happened yet? Does our faith in humanity wane if we see the person next to us achieve way more way more quickly, putting way less effort in, especially at being a good person? What keep us going and chugging along (even if it's at a snail's pace) towards our hopes and dreams?

If there ever was a time for an evolutionary collective consciousness shift, it would be right now. If we see a child being abused or taken advantage of by an angry and overzealous parent, we should say something. If we see somebody hurt on the street, or being trampled on by somebody trying to get past them instead of helping them, we should help that person. If there comes a time when our political system becomes so polarized, partisan and non-benefiting the vast many of us except for a chosen few and where inaction and deadlocks are the only occurrence, we must step up and take action. Sometimes it's the great things that happen fast and all at once.

I WILL ALWAYS CARRY THIS WITH ME AS A MADMAN FOR GOOD!!!!

ENTRY #141

2/12/12 – 7:27am

ANOTHER MANIFESTO OF A MADMAN FOR GOOD

If we are preparing for the future by living, learning and fighting for what we believe in, will the future automatically fall in our laps like guaranteed benefits from a contract? Do we have to picture and visualize what we want the world to be, and then learn, live and fight towards that goal? Should we prepare with purpose so we have constant motivation in our journey, which keeps us from getting stagnant and becoming depressed? Should we act with no purpose, because we think it's the right thing to do, because at least well be doing something even though we might not know why; but is that the point? Or do we prepare with purpose for the end goal we seek, and then work towards it even though we might not see the purpose of our actions right away, just that we are passionate and feel it's the right thing to do?

Acting with purpose, drive and determination will get us to the collective end goal we all seek. Acting with purpose, determination and learning along the way because we still have lessons, is the realization that will keep us on the right path.

I MUST ALWAYS ACT WITH PURPOSE AS A MADMAN FOR GOOD!!!!

ENTRY #142

2/12/12 – 7:46am

ANOTHER MANIFESTO OF A MADMAN FOR GOOD

How do we work towards a goal we all envision, if we don't know what the purpose of our individual actions are going to be in achieving that goal? How can we survive without purpose if we're just spinning our wheels all the time? If we see something we want, is it just somebody else telling us subconsciously or maybe consciously that we want this thing because our life wouldn't be the same without it, or is it a little voice within us that knows what we need, because it is us?

Acting with purpose for the big goals can be difficult if we've never done it before, especially if we're stuck in survival mode, just trying to have a place to sleep and food to eat. Acting with purpose is even more difficult if we are stuck in the thick muck of materialism, and know we should be working towards the goals we set for ourselves, but we would rather work towards a jet ski instead.

Unconscious actions towards materialism will lead us to emotional ruin. If we act with purpose and passion, the steps that will lead us to our goals will become much more vivid.

I NEED MUCH MORE OF THIS AS A MADMAN FOR GOOD!!!!

ENTRY #143

2/12/12 – 8:01am

ANOTHER MANIFESTO OF A MADMAN FOR GOOD

We must ask ourselves on a daily basis what we want to accomplish, how with determination we can realistically get there, and then go out and do it. We can't sit around for the perfect answer to fall out of the sky or seep up through the ground and right into our laps. We can however start each day with being thankful for what we have because there is always somebody who has it worse, and our problems pale in comparison to what they have to deal with on a daily basis. We can love the fact that we free ourselves from self-deprecation and beating ourselves up when we slow down, and see the real beauty in and of life.

Being thankful, and picturing its implications permeating through every thought and action we take will keep us motivated, and surrounded by thankfulness like a warm blanket on a cold winter night. We can go out and act with purpose when we attempt to heal the world.

I MUST REMIND MYSELF OF THIS EVERYDAY AS A MADMAN FOR GOOD!!!!

ENTRY #144

2/12/12 – 8:15am

ANOTHER MANIFESTO OF A MADMAN FOR GOOD

Starting the day with thankfulness, love for waking up, breathing and being alive helps our whole being tenfold. If we see a cause we really care about that makes passion just ooze out of our soul, being thankful will help us by helping somebody else. If there is an injustice that nobody seems to be doing anything about, (or at least not doing anything about fast enough) thankfulness will help correct this wrong by instilling in us the determination that we can face any foe, and we'll never back down.

Being relentless in pursuits of goodness, peace, justice, equality and consciousness raising can only be truly acted upon from a place of thankfulness for everything we have.

If we see somebody that needs help because they're being wronged, (whether they're the one being wronged or the one doing the wronging) we must realize that all people are at different consciousness levels within their own personal journeys; when we are thankful, everything else falls into place.

I MUST REMEMBER THIS IN ALL MY ACTIONS AS A MADMAN FOR GOOD!!!!

ENTRY #145

2/12/12 – 8:28am

ANOTHER MANIFESTO OF A MADMAN FOR GOOD

Do we have all the same basic goals in life, if we all have the same basic human needs? Do we all react differently to the same situation because we are all unique individual snowflakes, or because some of us are at different evolutionary levels? If we are all different and all the same at the same time, what hope can we have to unite by throwing off distractions? Is there a way to not get mad and thoroughly confused by the complexity of life, but to just accept it and work with what's there to build something better? Could this be the act of being thankful for what we have as the first thought we have when we wake up?

We need to love ourselves, in order to love others. We need to cultivate our soul, so we can help others grow. We need to fill up our own cup with thankfulness, love and passion for doing the right thing so we can fill others cups.

If we can put a smile on our face, there is a great chance we can put it on somebody else's as well. We need to treat ourselves special and be thankful, because there is nothing else that is even in the same realm of importance.

I MUST DELVE INTO THIS IDEA MORE AS A MADMAN FOR GOOD!!!!

ENTRY #146

2/13/12 – 8:19am

ANOTHER MANIFESTO OF A MADMAN FOR GOOD

Is there a way to avoid those days when we wake up and start thinking about all the worlds' ills and how they are too big and complex for us to handle? Is there a way to not think about it while not being oblivious to everything happening around us? Is this big and complex feeling about the world an illusion; is the world really as it seems? Or is it just a huge monstrosity that has many weaknesses because of its size and overreach?

Maybe we see the problem as being too big, my question is, why do we see it that way? Do we always have to realize the full breadth of something to take action for or against it?

We must understand humanity works because we continue to evolve and grow. Some issues are so big and will take a lot of work, but they can be fixed if everybody does their part. We must never say, "we will never find our path" or "I can't do anything about the world's problems." We must say, "If I keep my eyes open I will find my path, and I can change the world starting with this action right here?"

I MUST FIGURE THIS OUT AS A MADMAN FOR GOOD!!!!

ENTRY #147

2/13/12 – 8:32am

ANOTHER MANIFESTO OF A MADMAN FOR GOOD

There is a place for all of us in the bigger scheme of things. When we let go of our distractions to allow the real issues we face to reveal themselves, we will see that we can accomplish anything when we work together.

Think about it, issues like homelessness, joblessness, income equality, taxes and what functions government should perform would come to the forefront of our mind because we wouldn't be distractedly tearing each other down anymore. When we talk about what's at the heart and root of an issue, we'll find we all have a place, we all have a purpose, we all have a mission and will succeed when we all work together.

Not knowing our own place, mission, purpose or worth is a way we distract ourselves from what's really important; distractions sometimes do come from the inside, which can be tough to overcome. But, if we think about all the things we can and want to do, but won't or can't bring ourselves to the point of execution, we must remember we take our place and our mission for the planet when we allow ourselves to.

I MUST KEEP POUNDING THIS HOME AS A MADMAN FOR GOOD!!!!

ENTRY #148

2/13/12 – 8:46am

ANOTHER MANIFESTO OF A MADMAN FOR GOOD

Once we see ourselves as important enough to accomplish our goals, (or even set them in the first place) we have taken the first step towards forever. Once self-esteem creeps around and throughout our soul, we are ready and set to take on almost anything in the world. I say almost anything because just the mere fact that we don't know everything about everything, means all the worlds' issues might not have fully revealed themselves to us yet, so how can we handle them or say we can handle them, if we don't even fully know what they are?

There is no reason we should get worried about problems that we can't define; if ignorance is the thought of being scared of the big problems out there without knowing their contents, we would be feeding the problem. Ignorance can only exist when we have trepidation and fright about the unknown, which causes us to assume things. We must look inside ourselves at the issues affecting us and why they're happening. If we do, would we not be less ignorant of ourselves?

I MUST CONTINUOUSLY ASK THIS AS A MADMAN FOR GOOD!!!!

ENTRY #149

2/13/12 – 8:59am

ANOTHER MANIFESTO OF A MADMAN FOR GOOD

Starting the day thinking about what's possible is a lot more constructive then starting the day thinking about what's not possible because it's too difficult or has too many steps. Doing something for ourselves is a much more productive and fulfilling way to go through the day, instead of doing everything and using all our time to help others, making us feel miserable and not important for always doing for others and never doing for ourselves. It is an interesting thing to avoid inner battles by creating outer skirmishes; it's like this fire is burning inside us and we don't know what to do about it, so we try to avoid it and pretend it's not there. Instead of running away from the flames in our soul, we should accept them by finding out what feeds them and what doesn't.

It's about balance; we can always be more productive, constructive and loving human beings if we are less reactionary, ignorant and close minded because we are pro-active, think more critically and are more open to new ideas.

We have to open up to the world for it to open up to us.

I MUST REMEMBER EVERYBODY IS ON A DIFFERENT PART OF THEIR JOURNEY AS I JOURNEY AS A MADMAN FOR GOOD!!!!

ENTRY #150

2/13/12 – 9:12am

ANOTHER MANIFESTO OF A MADMAN FOR GOOD

If we rush around everywhere trying to admirably get things that we, our family or our friends might need done, life becomes no longer any fun. Is life really about how many million things we can accomplish in the shortest period of time? Is life about cramming so much into our day that the only time we have the ability to breathe is when we fall asleep at night? Or is life quite possibly about slowing down, taking a look around to assess the situation, and then deciding to act based on what will bring us the most satisfaction?

Maybe we can enjoy our short time on this amazing planet more if we tried figuring out why we were put here, and why people fight, argue and get distracted. We might find ourselves saying right now, "Figuring out why people do things is a huge undertaking with many parts, and would take a hell of a long time to decipher." The sooner we open up to all the world's possibilities, the sooner the answers will be revealed, creating an atmosphere of knowing. The simple fact of being open will help us enjoy our short planetary stop off by helping us be not scared of the unknown, but to be intrigued by it.

I MUST CONSTANTLY REMIND MYSELF OF THIS AS A MADMAN FOR GOOD!!!!

ENTRY #151

2/16/12 – 4:33pm

ANOTHER MANIFESTO OF A MADMAN FOR GOOD

There are issues many of us might never agree on, no matter how hard we try; such as certain moral beliefs and convictions we feel deep down in our heart to be true. However there are many more things we can agree on that often get overlooked, but it's the moral arguments that catch us up and get ingrained in our thinking.

People on opposite sides of the abortion issue might never see eye to eye because one side sees it at murder, while the other side sees it as a woman's right to choose what she does with her body; however, the 2 sides could agree on preventing the need for abortion in the first place.

People on opposite sides of the gun issue might never agree on how easy it should be for a law abiding person to buy as many guns and as much ammo as they want at one time; but they could agree on the fact that convicted violent criminals and mentally ill people shouldn't be able to buy guns or bullets at all.

People might not agree on how a person should come to live in this country, but they would agree that everybody deserves a fair shot at it.

We need to find common ground on the things we know we already agree on, and start the conversation from there. Then, once we're used to talking humanely and really listening to one another, we will have a fighting chance at defeating those much deeper, ingrained issues that are keeping us apart.

I MUST NEVER FORGET THIS AS A MADMAN FOR GOOD!!!!

ENTRY #152

2/16/12 – 4:49pm

ANOTHER MANIFESTO OF A MADMAN FOR GOOD

I don't know what's better, the fact that we can change our knowledge of the past by re-interpreting events, or that we can change the future by changing our present situation? It seems each idea is not independent, but might be mutually exclusive, and actually part of the same cycle.

By reinterpreting events of the past, we change our view of the present by rearranging what led up to the current time. Therefore, by changing our current view, we are inherently changing our future.

The idea is to not concentrate on any one point for too long, (obsessions can blind us) but to balance out the time we spend with each idea so we see how they feed off each other.

We can find a middle ground by slowing down, and taking time to reflect. What actions have we taken to get to this point? Have we learned the lessons of history? Are we currently still learning them?

Can we learn the lessons of significant historical events now so they aren't repeated 20 years down the road when everyone directly involved is either dead or can't remember?

We can learn these important lessons because the power to do so has always been with us even if we haven't realized it, we simply must lift the veils that are placed on us to cover our sight of them.

I MUST DECIPHER OUR COMMON GROUND SO I CAN START MY REAL WORK AS A MADMAN FOR GOOD!!!!

ENTRY #153

2/23/12 – 4:09pm

ANOTHER MANIFESTO OF A MADMAN FOR GOOD

Is coming together easy, or is it as hard as some of us make it out to be, depending on whatever news outlet we read, watch or listen to? Is coming together like trying to portray the problem as apples and oranges, or just portraying it as fruit? Are we all coming from completely different places, or are we from different smaller places that are all made up of the same big place?

Coming together is one of those things that is easy and hard at the same time; the concept of it might be simple, but the mechanics and operation are a completely different ballgame. We know we must see each other as equals who go after the same basic goals, but it's hard for some of us when we either don't see this at all, or when we're selfish enough to see only our own needs; basically it sounds good on paper, but could be very different in execution. A lot of trouble comes from not enough of us looking under the rug for the truth.

Maybe we don't know how to look deeply into something, or maybe we don't care. Maybe we need somebody who portrays the debt crisis as "not a big deal". Maybe we just need a universal list of truths we would all like to know, and things we could all agree on and just start from there.

THIS IS SOMETHING I MUST NEVER TIRE FROM WORKING ON AS A MADMAN FOR GOOD!!!!

ENTRY #154

2/24/12 – 4:16pm

ANOTHER MANIFESTO OF A MADMAN FOR GOOD

If home is where the heart is, we must ask ourselves, where is our heart? If home is what and where we make it, are we conscious enough in our decisions to make it so? If we're satisfied with our present situation or are comfortable with our surroundings, then what is the motivation for improvement? What pray tell are we supposed to do when all the cards are stacked against us? Are the challenges we face simply a test to see if we have the strength to fight for what our heart believes in?

When we start thinking outside the box, it can upset the comfortable situation, our "home" we have built for ourselves. Maybe we need to start the process by being thankful for what we have, so when challenges do arise, we will be ready to evolve because we have a solid starting point. "You don't have to go home, but you can't stay here" only means your home awaits, your home, not somebody else's. It is imperative we realize that home is whatever and wherever we make it because it's the foundation for our conscious evolution.

I MUST CONTINUE TO DEFINE THIS AS A MADMAN FOR GOOD!!!!

ENTRY #155

2/24/12 – 4:29pm

ANOTHER MANIFESTO OF A MADMAN FOR GOOD

Is it possible for a conservative and a liberal to get along for the sake of humanity? Is it necessary for the middle to veer to one side or the other just so they can be included in the discussion? Is any subject that can be deliberated made up of events and situations that are the same for all sides involved and which will be made abundantly clear once all the dust settles down?

Even though I feel that labels only serve to make us conform, I might be what some would call a liberal or a progressive. That fact however has no bearing on what I think might be a good war or a bad war; or what I may think about abortion, gun control or equal rights for people on all levels. My point is that liberals, conservatives, moderates, independents and whomever else are all after the same goal, which is betterment of our country. We must see that out basic human needs and desires are the same, the only difference is when and/or where we discover it.

I'M GONNA NEED LOTS OF HELP AS A MADMAN FOR GOOD!!!!

ENTRY #156

2/24/12 – 4:43pm

ANOTHER MANIFESTO OF A MADMAN FOR GOOD

When a governmental or business system is very powerful and seems to gain more influence with each passing day, how do we crack their armor? When a political system seems so stacked against the average person, how do we change how it functions? When a health system only seems to benefit the rich, while leaving the poor in ever increasing debt just to cling to its purse strings, how do we rearrange it? When a defense, military and police system is structured to keep the whole thing running, what chance do we have if we don't or won't see it all unfolding?

We need to keep our eyes open so we can spot the evidence that might bring the powerful down. We need to keep our ears open so we can hear the lies and double speak that is utilized to keep our minds closed. We need to keep talking and asking questions so we don't fall asleep, and so the "gatekeepers" don't get too comfortable.

Maybe all we need to do is stop, remember that they know they're lying to us, and we know they're lying to us, and all that's needed to defeat them, is starting the conversation with that fact.

I MUST CARRY THIS WITH ME TO STRENTHEN MY ARGUMENT AND REINFORCE MY "WHY" AS A MADMAN FOR GOOD!!!!

ENTRY #157

2/24/12 – 5:01pm

ANOTHER MANIFESTO OF A MADMAN FOR GOOD

If I proclaim myself as a madman, but for good, is there a way for us all to be mad people for good? If a mom is relentless in instilling in her kid a positive outlook and making them know their self-worth, doesn't that make her a mad mom for good? If a dad is relentless for instilling in his kid a feeling of working for what they need and want and for not doing anything half-ass, doesn't that make him a mad dad for good?

If a teacher takes real interest in their subject and helps their students to feel the excitement and wonderment that drives them to achieve more, doesn't that make them a mad teacher for good? If a doctor treats their patients as human beings with tolerance and humility so they always know they are in trusted hands at their most vulnerable moments, aren't they a mad doctor for good?

Maybe all we need to do to is find those positive consciousness raising activities that drive us, be thankful that we found them, and use that as motivation to heal the planet. Maybe we all have our part to play, we just need to remember our lines.

I MUST SHOW WE ALL HAVE THE MADMAN FOR GOOD GENE IN US AND CAN BRING IT OUT THROUGH OUR PASSIONS ON MY MISSION AS A MADMAN FOR GOOD!!!!

ENTRY #158

2/24/12 – 5:15pm

ANOTHER MANIFESTO OF A MADMAN FOR GOOD

Are there ways we can affect the same positive outcome for the planet if we all attack endemic problems from different directions? Is there a similarity between what the world thinks about us, and what we think about us? Is there a difference in intensity level for positive change from those of us with different occupations and/or consciousness levels? Are we all after the same thing, or do we just think we are?

Maybe the world will come to a point when all the racism, sexism and homophobic behavior that distract our good intentions won't even exist. Maybe we will go completely backwards and lose all the positive strides that we have made over the years. Maybe the fact that all people are created equal will actually be remembered and etched in stone, but maybe it won't.

The way we need to change our route so we don't get lost on a trip, is the same that can be said for life's journey. We all have differences, and we all have sames. The key to our positive evolution as a species, is deciding which way will bring the most of us together.

I NEED TO NEVER STOP ASKING MYSELF THIS AS A MADMAN FOR GOOD!!!!

ENTRY #159

3/1/12 – 4:10pm

ANOTHER MANIFESTO OF A MADMAN FOR GOOD

If we believe in a certain religion, do we have the right to proselytize to others without them seeking us out? If we believe somebody is going down the wrong and moral path, will we be able to unequivocally state what the right and moral path is for them, or anybody else for that matter? Does it matter if the recipient is alive or dead? What if they had deceased relatives and/or friends that didn't know about it? Is it ever okay to baptize somebody without their knowledge, let alone without their presence? What makes somebody think they can get baptized on anyone else's behalf beside their own?

Maybe it comes from the thought that their religion is the only true religion, and anybody else that doesn't think so will burn in eternal hellfire. Maybe it comes from the fact they are trying to control the one baptized for their own devious purposes. Maybe the purpose is that if the person was alive, they would never be a convert. There have been forced religious conversions throughout our history, and if we learn about how they never worked, we will learn that all of us control our own minds.

I MUST CONTINUE TO REALIZE THIS AS A MADMAN FOR GOOD!!!!

ENTRY #160

3/1/12 – 4:23pm

ANOTHER MANIFESTO OF A MADMAN FOR GOOD

If forced conversions don't change a person's soul, will speaking with them about what they believe, then what we believe bring about the ultimate compromise we seek? If we made somebody do something exactly the way we wanted and it worked out, why aren't there robots roaming the streets looking for work? What may be the thinking behind the force? Is there deep thought, or is it all action now and questions later?

It's not right to disturb the dead because of a living fantasy that some of us believe to be true within the deepest depths of their soul. The words rest in peace don't mean squat if a living person does a whole bunch of stuff for a dead person, which is really for the living anyway, not the deceased. We may not be able to figure out every fascinating fact on the planet during our short visit here, but we can enjoy what little time we have. Why waste time worrying about what other living people think, let alone what other dead people might think.

Starting the dialogue between us with where we agree, and then moving forward from there, may stop forced conversions all together, forever.

I NEED TO HONE THIS DOWN AS A MADMAN FOR GOOD!!!!

ENTRY #161

3/1/12 – 4:37pm

ANOTHER MANIFESTO OF A MADMAN FOR GOOD

Why are we so afraid to talk to each other about real issues if we have so much in common as human beings? Is there a reason the old saying is in effect "you never speak of two things, politics and religion"? Is that saying there because we are afraid of what we or someone else might say? Or is it because we see politics and religion as off limits in favor of meaningless drivel we can regurgitate to any stranger on the street?

Maybe because politics and religion have countless viewpoints dealing with an issue, nervousness about offending the other person enters into the equation, and causes us to not talk. Maybe we haven't thought deeply enough to fully comprehend the political and religious ramifications of ignorance.

Maybe political thought is on the outside and religious thought is on the inside; and even though they might balance each other out inside of us while we're trying to figure out life, there still might be exceptions. We can talk about anything to anybody at any time so long as we also listen.

I MUST REMEMBER THIS AS A MADMAN FOR GOOD!!!!

ENTRY #162

3/1/12 – 4:49pm

ANOTHER MANIFESTO OF A MADMAN FOR GOOD

We might never know what we're able to accomplish if we don't make the attempt. Just as a flower can't bloom without sunlight or water, neither can a human being grow without love and understanding. There might be a tied up beast inside of us, just waiting to bust out of its self-inflicted shackles the moment we show it how to untie a knot. We might not realize that we are the same as each other, only different in external looks, ethnicity and culture. We may not seem like we have the ability to bring people together, but we do.

The only thing stopping us from upending our unjust and corrupt system and forcing it to work for 99% of us instead of the sharks at the top of the food chain, is us. If we can't come together because of the distractions placed on us like an "all-knowing" witch casting a spell, we have to slow down and think about why we are doing things the hard way, and not the easy way by critically thinking about them. If we never make the attempt to throw off distractions, we will always be floating around looking for something to grasp onto. If we do try to shake off distractions, we will know what's bullshit, and what's not.

I MUST INSCRIBE THIS INTO MY CREED AS A MADMAN FOR GOOD!!!!

ENTRY #163

3/1/12 – 5:01pm

ANOTHER MANIFESTO OF A MADMAN FOR GOOD

Is there a question in this day and age that suggests something is going on other than what it's being made out to be? Is there a method for figuring out not only that the wool is being pulled over our eyes, but why and how pervasive? Are media outlets just machines that are created to crank out whatever crap they think might be important at any given moment? Are they designed to dissuade and/or distract any rational or critical thought we might have; or are they both of those things, but with a few nuggets of truth thrown in just to keep us on our toes?

Whenever we get bored with our station in life, we need to look for new ways to spend our time; the question if we can't figure out our priorities isn't how do we hurry up to catch them or how do we slow down to see them, it's why are we getting bored? Is there anything that will stimulate our thought process? Is it possible to make positive social change and bring justice if we concentrate on being bored, as opposed to coming to the table with solutions that will help society?

We might end up where we never expect, but we can expect to get there.

I MUST KEEP ASKING THIS AS A MADMAN FOR GOOD!!!!

ENTRY #164

3/5/12 – 11:01am

ANOTHER MANIFESTO OF A MADMAN FOR GOOD

If we are creatures of our surroundings, do we go through a species change when we move around? Is there a possibility our surroundings can help or hinder our evolution, but not be the most important factor in it? Is it true that when we change our thoughts and actions that it doesn't matter where in life it happens, just that it happens, especially if we are floating on a sea of uncertainty?

If we want to fix our surroundings, we have to adjust our thinking. We must organize in our minds what's important to us. We must try to figure out what's best for us and humanity, so we can give to ourselves and to humanity.

Writing this book isn't easy; it's hard for me sometimes to organize my thoughts in such a way that they would actually make sense when I put them on paper. The thing is though; it's my priority, will and purpose to accomplish this organizational task. For when I do, I will attempt to be the shining example of how humanity should be to each other. Of course, now that I think about it, maybe I'm already there, and maybe, so are you!

I MUST CONSTANTLY REINFORCE MY PURPOSE AS A MADMAN FOR GOOD!!!!

ENTRY #165

3/6/12 – 8:05am

ANOTHER MANIFESTO OF A MADMAN FOR GOOD

Is it possible that the people at the top controlling us with their distractions fully know the implications of their actions? Do they grasp the present situation where millions upon millions of us feel helpless and hopeless that we will ever get ahead? Do the people at the top become weary and antsy because when all is said and done all they will be able to show for their lives are a bunch of material goods, meaningless friendships and partnerships? Are they prepared for a backlash when their scheme is uncovered and their distractions are completely dispelled?

Maybe the people at the top do know what they're doing by keeping us fighting amongst ourselves, because they think we won't bite the hand that feeds us. Maybe they only see the short term gains that line their pockets with occasional blood money, and they don't see the long term consequences of a docile public who fully and completely wakes up to their own reality as well as the worlds.

Finding out the people at the top's power is based on an illusion will give us the motivation to make our power authentic by being examples of the change we want to see.

I MUST FIND THIS OUT AS A MADMAN FOR GOOD!!!!

ENTRY #166

3/6/12 – 8:19am

ANOTHER MANIFESTO OF A MADMAN FOR GOOD

When we first become aware of our honest and non-distracted reality, will we see what needs to be done to heal the planet? Will all the crap we've been fighting over just melt away because we'll know it's not important who marries whom, who does what in their own home or what God or higher power a person happens to believe in? Will we see the reality that's before us and move forward in making it better for all of us? Will we see what has been swept under the rug, but instead of making sure it doesn't get covered up again; we simply go out and buy a bigger rug from the same people that put down the original rug in the first place?

Maybe we will react to the "uncovering" by helping and healing people so they can discover all the important aspects of life. Maybe we will see everything out in the open and see it as causing more distraction then before, forcing us to cower in the corner and yearn for the day when we didn't have to think of what's important, and when somebody else told us how we should conduct our lives. Maybe we'll be a little hesitant at first, (it's very different from our norm) but when we fully embrace the unknown, we will know we have the ability to shape it. In the unknown lies our true potential.

I MUST INSTILL THIS IN MYSELF AND OTHERS AS A MADMAN FOR GOOD!!!!

ENTRY #167

3/16/12 – 8:34am

ANOTHER MANIFESTO OF A MADMAN FOR GOOD

Is boredom the key in breaking out of the shackles that have been placed on us by multiple sources? Does feeling like nothing matters give us the strength to hunt and seek out what does matter? Is simply not being satisfied with our current situation enough to get us off our ass to do something about it?

They key to any game is a good offense and a good defense; we must go out there and uncover, release, find, locate and bring up and out all injustices committed by public and private officials in power. We must defend ourselves when our discoveries start to ruffle feathers, kink armor, and when the powerful crack down on the powerless. We have to stop and think however, we might have a good offense that really takes it to the "power players" and "money changers" and upsets their power. We might have a good defense by not letting bad energy and/or distractions stop us from our main mission of healing the planet and all its inhabitants. But, if we don't play together as one cohesive unit, we won't be successful in our mission; all we'll have is a lot of good sounding talk from a lot of singular people. Life is a team sport; we all succeed when we all succeed.

THIS IS A MAIN ARTERY FOR ME AS A MADMAN FOR GOOD!!!!

ENTRY #168

3/7/12 – 7:54 am

ANOTHER MANIFESTO OF A MADMAN FOR GOOD

When a government is trending away or attempting to trend away from communism, socialism or some other ism no longer accepted and feared, what are the signs that it has disappeared? Is there a fool proof way to tell if a current incarnation of a head of state is completely different than the one before? Does communism ever disappear, or does it just evolve into something different? Does socialism ever die completely, or does it weave certain aspects of itself into most current governmental systems we have?

When a person serves as President then Prime Minister and then President again, is there an obvious conflict of interest? When a government official leaves their post and goes into the business world dealing with the same stuff their former job required them to deliberate on, then jumps right back into a similar government position as before, is there a conflict of interest? Maybe some of us feel like we can pull the wool over other people's eyes because of their short term attention span. Maybe they feel they can distract people from what's really important by keeping them fighting amongst themselves. Maybe the kinks in the armor are already there, we just have to aim for them.

I MUST LOOK INTO THIS AS A MADMAN FOR GOOD!!!!

ENTRY #169

3/7/12 – 8:08am

ANOTHER MANIFESTO OF A MADMAN FOR GOOD

Are there businesses, government functions or government offices that should never be privatized? Should education change from a system that accepts everybody and uses educating the young as a model of success, to a system that only accepts those who can pay, and uses profits as a model for success? Should a prison system change from what's best for the prisoners rehabilitation, to how meals, health care and educational opportunities can be skimped on, and locking up as many people as possible so the private prison owners can keep making money hand over fist? Should the health care system move from being profit driven, making as much money off the backs of its patients as possible until they croak, to one where everybody gets treated regardless of income, causing profit to be taken completely out of the equation, which in turn would bring the price down.

There are certain things that should always stay private. We should be able to start a business and become successful when we put in the hard work and don't dehumanize anybody along the way. There are some things however that should never be done for profit. When we make money off people being smarter, getting punished or getting healed, we forget about the people.

I MUST NEVER FORGET THIS AS A MADMAN FOR GOOD!!!!

ENTRY #170

3/7/12 – 8:23am

ANOTHER MANIFESTO OF A MADMAN FOR GOOD

Would the founding fathers ever have imagined a presidential candidate might have to raise one billion dollars just to win? Would Ben Franklin have been okay with candidates separating us into the faithful and the heathens? Would Thomas Jefferson have given his approval to privatizing schools and only making them available to the upper crust of society? Would John Hancock have put down his famous signature if he thought that the country he helped to design, would one day be faulting its design and praising it at the same time (whichever proved to be more politically advantageous).

Maybe when we converse with each other we should remember that above all else the "framers" valued critical thought and asking questions; maybe their intentions with the constitution was for us to think for ourselves, and to create a living document that can evolve with the times. Maybe they wanted all people to be free from tyranny, foreign and domestic. Maybe they wanted us to come together and realize that we are our brother's and sister's keeper and it means exactly that, that we take care of our own, our own human race.

What are we waiting for?

I MUST REINFORCE THIS ALL THE TIME AS A MADMAN FOR GOOD!!!!

ENTRY #171

3/8/12 – 4:15pm

ANOTHER MANIFESTO OF A MADMAN FOR GOOD

When laws were passed to end institutionalized racism, did they change what was in our hearts? If it was no longer okay for us to discriminate against one another because some of us might look, think or believe differently, did we just all of a sudden wake up and say hey, I guess I shouldn't do that anymore? Where is the line drawn between our actions and our thoughts? Can a law ever change a thought or a belief?

Maybe there is always a way around a law, no matter how strict it seems. Maybe some of our ingrained racial beliefs taught and inherited over generations need a lot more in-depth and personal work to fix than any law could provide. Maybe in an effort to look past the beliefs some of us hold, it's important to see ourselves in somebody else's shoes. We should take a day, and concentrate on what's really important to us. Then think about what's important to the person we profess to hate. Then, when we realize that it's basically the same, we have taken the first step in uniting us all. Once we see each other as having the same basic human needs as one another, we have won half the battle.

I MUST ALWAYS FILL THE WORLD WITH GOOD ENERGY AS A MADMAN FOR GOOD!!!!

ENTRY #172

3/2/12 – 4:30pm

ANOTHER MANIFESTO OF A MADMAN FOR GOOD

What are the issues keeping us from coming together as a people? Is it racism, sexism, religious persecution, or some other ism we could think up? Can these issues be overcome in our lifetime? Can these issues be discussed in earnest in our lifetime? Can anything be accomplished with how polarized we have become? Is now our only opportunity, or do we have as much time as we need?

We have many issues to work out before we can all unite and rise up to throw off all our collective oppressors. If we want to unite and make a better life for us all, we have to stop degrading people because of the color of their skin. If we want to unite we have to stop degrading people because they happen to be a man or a woman. If we want to unite we have to stop degrading others because they are lesbian, gay, bisexual or transgendered. We must definitely stop degrading people based on what "higher power" they believe in or don't believe in.

Most importantly however, we must stick to our collective goals of overcoming all distractions so the real work can begin.

I MUST KEEP THIS AT THE FOREFRONT OF THE CONVERSATION AS A MADMAN FOR GOOD!!!!

ENTRY #173

3/8/12 – 4:45pm

ANOTHER MANIFESTO OF A MADMAN FOR GOOD

Once all the issues are on the table and out in the open that we as a people need to overcome so we can unite, then what? Once we start talking <u>with</u> each other instead of <u>at</u> each other, how do we progress from there? Once we are able to see the distractions pushed on us and how they cloud our judgment, how do we come together once the rhetoric has died down? Once we become engaged in humane discussion, how do we bond together as one force against the heavy handed elites that have kept us down for so long?

Maybe once we start talking about our prejudices and thoughts, and we overcome all the "brainwashing" we might have endured, we might be able to come up with a plan for positive world evolution. Maybe once our thoughts are unclouded about the "elites", "fat cats", and "big wigs", (whatever you want to call them) we can see why these distractions are placed on us. We might even be able to change a few skeptics' minds along the way. If we are about to decide what's best for the world, we should look in the mirror. When people are asking what we are thinking, we might give them a completely random answer, but at least we're talking to them. That's a start.

THIS WILL ALWAYS BE TRUE IF I STAY HONEST AND TRUE TO MYSELF AS A MADMAN FOR GOOD!!!!

ENTRY #174

3/13/12 – 8:14am

ANOTHER MANIFESTO OF MADMAN FOR GOOD

If we find ourselves cruising along without a care in the world, and something happens that gives us an explanation that something completely different is going on than we expected to happen, what will we do? If we get clues that something is going on right under the surface, just waiting to be released into the open air, will we lift the veil and fully see what's been covered up? Will we be frightened of all the things that might be revealed? Will we be excited that some of these issues are being brought to light so they can finally be discussed in the open? Will we be uneasy because the comfortable ruts we have built for ourselves might not be comfortable anymore because of the truth? Or will it be a combination of all three, excitement, fear and uneasiness meant to inform and enlighten us whether we want it to or not?

Maybe there are things we can't explain if we use the standard double speak that comes down from on high. Maybe some of us don't want the rug to be lifted revealing what's underneath, because not only will knowledge be gained about what the "power brokers" do, we will also learn what we are made of as humans

I MUST CONSTANTLY DELVE INTO THIS AS A MADMAN FOR GOOD!!!!

ENTRY #175

3/13/12 – 8:27am

ANOTHER MANIFESTO OF A MADMAN FOR GOOD

When we see what's under the rug, behind the curtain or when we read between the lines, we might get scared, grow uneasy and become excited, but when do we act? How much evidence of wrong doing needs to be produced before we get out of our chairs and say enough is enough? Is the turning point the same or different for all of us? Will we stand tall, together and united against the powers that want to keep us fighting amongst each other so we'll be distracted from what they're doing? Or will we continue to argue, disagree and sometimes brawl over how to stand up, and what to stand up for?

Maybe the idea is to act sooner than later so the problem doesn't get way worse; respond rather than react. Maybe we all want to change the system so it benefits us all, but we want to help people like "us" first. Maybe the ultimate fuck you is the fact the "money changers" and "wall street barons" know we will find out they are screwing us; not only will we find out about the act of getting screwed, but also how hard and fast. They know we will eventually find out what they're up to. They plan on us having all the evidence of their deeds in front of us and in plain sight, but keep us too distracted and fighting amongst each other to do anything about it. Let's prove them wrong.

I MUST CONSTANTLY REINFORCE THIS AS A MADMAN FOR GOOD!!!!

ENTRY #176

3/13/12 – 8:42am

ANOTHER MANIFESTO OF A MADMAN FOR GOOD

If we decide to act by ourselves to create a symbol with very strong political and social implications, will it have effect, if only one person is standing by as witness? What if the symbol is strong like exploding a building or killing a head of state, would it matter as much if nobody is standing behind the gunman in support? Even though a conscious act might be violent, can it ever be meant for good? Is a violent or unwarranted act to upset the status quo still just a symbol of getting past rage into action if the perpetrator was its only supporter? Or would it have much deeper and permeating qualities if there were thousands, even millions of people supporting the act?

Maybe there are actions that must be taken to prolong humanity and continue our positive evolution as a species. Maybe such events as taking certain people out of office who are perpetrators of some of our worst societal ills, won't affect the bigger picture. Offices can be replaced right along with office holders. That's why to really positively change things, we need to throw off distractions, not fight amongst each other for stupid reasons, unite, rise up and show the "powers that be" that there are going to be some changes around here!

THIS IS SOMETHING I HAVE TO MOTIVATE AS A MADMAN FOR GOOD!!!!

ENTRY #177

3/14/12 – 8:17am

ANOTHER MANIFEST OF A MADMAN FOR GOOD

What is the determining factor in an election; is it facts, popularity, money, ideas, lies or is it something completely different? Might the determining factor in an election at any level be as simple as whose turn is it? Might somebody feel pre-ordained or just feel like it's their turn to take over? Do they feel the same pains as the people that vote for them? Or are they just acting like they give a shit and can sympathize, when in actuality they could care less about the people because it's their turn to be president?

It might all come back to the lies. If the politicians know they're lying to the people, and the people know they're being lied to by the politicians, but neither side does anything to change the situation, then they deserve each other. But, if the people can pick through the crap and see the lies for what they are, (just a means of getting a person into a position of power they think they deserve) then they can do something about it. Lies are told so often they seem true after so many repetitions, and that is what politicians count on. So the next time we go into a voting box we should remember these words, everybody lies and sometimes for completely opposite reasons, finding what their motive is for doing so, is what will swing our evolution in a positive direction.

I MUST CONTINUE TO FIGURE THIS OUT AS A MADMAN FOR GOOD!!!!

ENTRY #178

3/14/12 – 8:32am

ANOTHER MANIFESTO OF A MADMAN FOR GOOD

Does it seem like whoever has the loudest voice is the only one that gets heard? Is it true that those of us who yell, scream, swear, stomp or pound the loudest are the people we're supposed to turn to when our country is in trouble? Are Junior High elections for class president and an "adult" election for a country's president any different at their root? Will drowning out the voice of your opponent guarantee a victory? How long does it have to be where loud people with so-so ideas win and the quieter people with really great ideas don't?

Since all sides of an electorate know that to win an election you have to get your platform out to as many people as possible, the idea might be to yell and scream so the platform projects out to a bigger crowd. But, if one of us has some really great ideas for not only fixing economies and putting people back to work, but fixing the environment and education system as well, we should always hear them out, even if they don't shout it from the rooftops. These ideas might take some critical thinking on our part, but when we open up to them, we will wonder how we ever thought a bad idea at full volume ever sounded good.

I WILL INVESTIGATE THIS AS A MADMAN FOR GOOD!!!!

ENTRY #179

3/14/12 – 8:48am

ANOTHER MANIFESTO OF A MADMAN FOR GOOD

If getting over the distractions placed on us by the "powerbrokers" is only the first step, what's next? Once we see that we have a lot more in common then we don't, where do we go from there?

The first step is getting past all the distractions placed on us, because most of us are in the same boat and we have much more in common than not. Maybe the way forward is starting the conversation; within those talks however are things we might never agree on. If we start talking about what we agree on and have a humanistic understanding of each other while we do it, then we can delve into the deeper problems. If we start from where we don't agree, it can delve into personal attacks, and then the one who wins the argument is the one who yells the loudest.

Do we want a political world where it just gets more polarized by the day, where the richest and loudest person wins because nobody is critically thinking and asking questions about what somebody might actually be saying? Or do we want a world where people can find common ground and use it as a springboard to fix real problems? Our positive human evolution depends on the answer.

I MUST NEVER STOP PUSHING AS A MADMAN FOR GOOD!!!!

ENTRY #180

3/16/12 – 4:25pm

ANOTHER MANIFESTO OF A MADMAN FOR GOOD

The winds of change are howling and calling us to action. Are we ready as a species, as a people and as a world community to answer the charge? Are we going to be able to get past our petty differences (or as I like to call them distractions) so we all can unite? Will we able to set aside our old prejudices because we will see them for what they are, ignorant thoughts meant to block us from the truth? Or will we let our emotions get the better of us, continue to be scared of what we don't know about and have a meaningless existence because we only care about bettering our own situation? Will we be able to get past all the shit we have shoveled onto our own path? Will the stench be so over-powering that it prevents us from moving forward?

I don't know what the future is going to hold, whether we will be able to overcome the self-inflicted adversity we have placed on ourselves is above my pay grade. But I do know this, every time we feel like cracking up because everything seems like its stacked against us, we just have to remember, it is us as in ALL OF US that control our own destiny. It is up to us whether we want to spend our time building people up or tearing them down.

I MUST ALWAYS BE COGNIZANT OF THIS AS A MADMAN FOR GOOD!!!!

ENTRY #181

3/16/12 – 4:51pm

ANOTHER MANIFESTO OF A MADMAN FOR GOOD

Treating everybody as we would like to be treated are words to live by. Whether we are jerks or nice to somebody depends on our outlook. If we treat people like crap, then we probably feel like crap. If we treat somebody nice, then we probably feel nice. This isn't rocket science. We must feel good about ourselves so we can make others feel good about themselves, or else we might find ourselves being jerks all the time.

I have said it often in this book and I will say it again because it deserves to be said, once we see others as having the same human needs as ourselves, then the real work begins. We will see that others go through the same trials and tribulations that we do, and in turn we will want to treat them nice because we have gone through the same crap, and we can sympathize. We can also be empathetic towards them because we'll be able to not only walk in their shoes, but be able to see the world through their eyes. Sympathy and empathy are not weaknesses, they are the energy and strength we must find so we can band together and make the changes that will better us all. This will happen and this can happen once we learn to treat ourselves kind.

I MUST REINFORCE THIS EVERYDAY THROUGH ALL MY ACTIONS AS A MADMAN FOR GOOD!!!!

ENTRY #182

3/19/12 – 9:47am

ANOTHER MANIFESTO OF A MADMAN FOR GOOD

What if police, military and others in positions of authority are not trying to scam the public and lock them into a conspiratorial plan to dominate the world, they're just ignorant? What if these agents and gate keepers for the "powers that be" are not trying to control the people, but are ignorant of the people, and get scared because the people can gather in huge numbers and can rise up against them at any time? What would happen if the "guardians" one day became not ignorant to why they are given orders to control the masses, and realize they're actually a part of the masses, just controlled in a different way?

There is an old thought that says Nazi soldiers shouldn't be blamed for the horrible atrocities they committed because they were just taking orders; did it not register in their minds what they were told to do, or did they feel a deep passion within to carry it out? Or somehow were they forced to be ignorant so they wouldn't step out of line?

The goal of all police, military and other security is control. When they realize that the control they are being told to carry out is actually controlling them and keeping them in line, they will throw of their shackles and be free.

I MUST VIGOROUSLY PURSUE THIS AS A MADMAN FOR GOOD!!!!

ENTRY #183

3/19/12 – 10:00am

ANOTHER MANIFESTO OF A MADMAN FOR GOOD

When "gatekeepers" and "guardians" realize their place and function allows the machine to run in the first place, will they just automatically move over to the side of justice?

Will they flock to the all-important people's movement for positive social and political change and consciousness raising?

Will they flock the other way and join or start a militia bent on weeding certain undesirables out of society and overthrowing the government?

It seems there are three options a recently enlightened authority figure can do: They can demand justice from the government on the left; they can ignore the new finding all together and continue their work in becoming more ignorant as the days go by in the middle, or they can demand freedom from the government on the right.

See any similarities here? The left wants justice and the right wants freedom, and they both want it from the government. Justice includes the freedom to go about your day and not get harassed.

Freedom includes the ability to have justice for the wrong doings that have been perpetrated.

So when police or others get enlightened to their real mission and don't ignore it, the two paths they can choose from are almost identical; this should be the starting point, because of the clear picture it provides, from the right or the left.

I MUST FOCUS ON THIS AS A MADMAN FOR GOOD!!!!

ENTRY #184

3/19/12 – 10:14am

ANOTHER MANIFESTO OF A MADMAN FOR GOOD

When we as a people begin to enter the enlightening process we might be scared, but is it excitement as well? Is it actual fear of the unknown that drives our thoughts, or is it just unknown, so it depends on us and our life experience to gauge ourselves on what we feel fear is? What if we could just immediately change the world and not tell anybody that we did? What would be different when we woke up? We all can be scared of the unknown, but since everybody knows and is on this same level playing field, shouldn't it be less difficult?

What if all this struggle were going through right now as a species is just a test for something much bigger that needs to be done, and if we can't get past all our petty crap now, how can we expect to even track the bigger problems? When we are born, none of us know what the outside world is made of and the reasons for why things happen. We might be scared because everything is so new, but we move forward in our learning experiences because we want to know certain things and we want to have fun. As is life, none of us know what will happen in the future because it's all unknown, but the more we move forward, the more we figure out and the more connected we will realize we already were.

I MUST BRING THIS CONCEPT TO LIGHT AS A MADMAN FOR GOOD!!!!

ENTRY #185

3/19/12 – 10:27pm

ANOTHER MANIFESTO OF A MADMAN FOR GOOD

If we know what our profession, station or mission in life is supposed to be, we can prove to the world that we can make positive change through our actions and not just talk about them; but mostly we will be able to prove to ourselves that we can accomplish our goals in the first place. If we don't prove to ourselves that we can accomplish our goals, but instead try to go out and change the world anyway, we will fail because we didn't believe it was possible, so we didn't put in the full energy required.

Now, if we believe we can do something towards accomplishing our goals and towards positive world change, our passions start brewing up all the possibilities and directions we could go with it. We might start to see things not fully understood yet, that become more vibrant and pouring forth their answers the more we look for them.

We must believe in ourselves. We must believe in the strength and love that simultaneously makes up the human character and we must love others because we can see them within ourselves.

I know I said before that one person can't change the world. Well, if enough of us started treating ourselves kindly, we would want to treat others kindly as well. Once we treat others kindly, we are halfway to our goal of engulfing the world in love, peace, humanism and accountability. Once this peace, love and humanism occurs, we will be able to band together and accomplish that proverbial next step because enough of us believed in ourselves, and believed we could change the world. Be kind.

I MUST SAY THIS OVER AND OVER IN MY HEAD AS A MADMAN FOR GOOD!!!!

ENTRY#186

3/20/12 – 7:52am

ANOTHER MANIFESTO OF A MADMAN FOR GOOD

If there is an ideological battle currently underway that only gets more defined over time, how will we react amidst continuous understanding? When confronted with ideas that not only differ from ours but aim to crash our world around us, will we fight back? Will we compromise? Will we runaway?

Many of us want to save the world and make it a more conscious place, but might not believe in our hearts that we can.

I'm telling you right now that everybody has this consciousness in them, just some of us don't know how to use it, (or even know it's there in the first place) or we do we know about it but get distracted by the stimuli that bombard us every day meant to keep us numb to the real problems in society.

We must wake up. It might take a while, it might not happen instantly or in the way we expect, but we must never give up. It's as if our foot fell asleep; we can't yell at it to wake it up, or even pour water on it.

We must walk on the foot with pins and needles at first; but the more we walk on it, the more comfortable and easier it gets. Such is the same with life.

We just have to put one foot in front of the other and keep moving forward. When we wake up to the inner strength we've always had to change the world and raise its consciousness, the why is sometimes more important than the how.

I MUST ALWAYS KEEP THIS ISSUE ON MY FRONT BURNER AS A MADMAN FOR GOOD!!!!

ENTRY #187

3/26/12 – 9:34am

ANOTHER MANIFESTO OF A MADMAN FOR GOOD

One of the most difficult parts about achieving our collective goals through humanism and accountability is coming to agreement on terms. How do we reach an agreement, if we have a million different opinions designed to produce a million different results with a million sinister aims behind them? How do we correlate them all? Do we just say "fuck it, it's too hard to even make an attempt, I'm so locked into my own survival that I know if I step out of line and point out all the hypocrisy in front of me, I won't be in a comfortable rut anymore designed to keep me blind, dumb and full?"

Or do we say "you know what, we can do this? I'm tired of being lied to, and knowing I'm being lied to by a liar who has conscious purpose and knowledge of the lies they are spewing at me. I'm tired of knowing the game is rigged, and knowing that the people who are doing the rigging know exactly what they're doing. I'm tired, I'm antsy and I'm ready to act. I'm ready to do something with a loving heart and positive thoughts. I can't fail because everybody is waiting for the right moment because they have the same thoughts within them."

I MUST ALWAYS WORK ON THIS AS A MADMAN FOR GOOD!!!!

ENTRY #188

3/26/12 – 9:48am

ANOTHER MANIFESTO OF A MADMAN FOR GOOD

Deciding on a way forward, a course of action or finding purpose is subjective; by virtue of being human we might have completely different definitions. We need to ask ourselves what it means to be human. What course of action would best serve all of humanity, what purpose would it serve and why would we want to do it in the first place?

Once we have our own, solo-inner thought out answers to these questions, then we can share them with others; then we compare, contrast and co-mingle. First comes the thought and then comes the action; because if the action came first, we wouldn't know anything about why it was occurring. If we think our own thoughts about what actions we want to take, then the want to share them will be overwhelming.

I MUST HELP PEOPLE WITH THIS AS WELL AS MYSELF AS A MADMAN FOR GOOD!!!!

ENTRY #189

3/26/12 – 10:00am

ANOTHER MANIFESTO OF A MADMAN FOR GOOD

If we feel important to ourselves and give off the confidence it produces, would others pick up on it? Would they see or overhear, "oh, this person is important and we should listen to them, pay attention and take in everything they say because their words are infallible, listen to them speak, oh my?" Or would some of us take in all the information, eject what isn't useful, and carry on with the good stuff throughout our day where we continue to hunt and search for more good stuff tidbits?

We can produce confidence, real or unreal to prove or un-prove just about anything and everything, just like a survey or a poll does with numbers. The key is to be confident and strong but kind and open to new thoughts at the same time. The balance is difficult, nobody said life was going to be easy; but the end result of listening and keeping what is useful and rejecting the un-useful is what makes our journey possible. Only when we are confident enough to love ourselves, can we love enough to produce confidence in others.

I MUST ALWAYS REMEMBER THIS AS A MADMAN FOR GOOD!!!!

ENTRY #190

3/26/12 – 10:14am

ANOTHER MANIFESTO OF A MADMAN FOR GOOD

There are many ingrained cycles within our societal existence, are they always spinning out of control with no end in sight? Can love and understanding break cycles of violence, hate and ignorance? Can critical thinking break cycles of not asking questions? Can accountability break cycles of blanket immunity overtly and covertly? Can humanism end wars? Can love overcome hate?

We all have thoughts about how to fix things in the world. Even if we have plans to improve things, we might know what would happen after they improve, but what is it that stops these thoughts from becoming actions? What is it that can get us all riled up and pissed off, but stops us short from doing something about it? Are we wrapped up in such a big cycle, that most people are stuck in that same collective cycle? Or are we our own little cycles that bump into other little cycles, but can unite for important purposes in the "larger" cycle.

We all have a purpose, we just have to remember everybody else does too.

I MUST CONTINUOUSLY WORK TO REFINE THIS IDEA AS A MADMAN FOR GOOD!!!!

ENTRY #191

3/27/12 – 8:09am

ANOTHER MANIFESTO OF A MADMAN FOR GOOD

From the moment we wake up till the moment we go to sleep at night, we might be at the point where we know we're going to get bombarded from every angle telling us how we should live and how we should act. We might be at the point where it's expected that what we're being told is either lies or persuasion, designed to bring us over to somebody else's way of thinking. We might be at the place where we find this book that our friend told us about or we might have found online, that says there might be a different way; the book might say that with everything out there telling us how to think, its purpose for us is to get past distractions and start thinking for ourselves. The book might even point out how to get past these distractions, who is designing them and that their purpose is total control and ignorance amongst the population.

If there be such a book, TV show, movie or even a pamphlet, I suggest you read or watch it. It might be for our highest good as well as the authors. It might be what you're looking for; it might be what we're all looking for.

I MUST ALWAYS KEEP UP THE SEARCH AS A MADMAN FOR GOOD!!!!

ENTRY #192

3/27/12 – 8:20am

ANOTHER MANIFESTO OF A MADMAN FOR GOOD

An item, book, magazine, pamphlet or maybe just a person on the side of the road might be the turning point in our evolutionary journey. Our eyes might already be open, but we can still be taught how to see; we must stay conscious and open for any opportunity that may come before us.

We might be at a place where we know about the problems of the world, (wars, corruption, genocide, etc….). We might know how the system is rigged against us. We might even talk about how we all got to do something about it because we know what the problems are. Are the problems too ingrained and the "controllers" too powerful and influential because they've been in power to long for us to do anything about? Do we see all these problems and sometimes even how and why they are happening, but still do nothing about them for fear of reprisal or revenge? Comfortable surroundings can be hard to overcome; they can keep us from stepping into the fray. The important thing to remember though is this; the people laying the distractions down, plan on us being mixed up and unsure of what or how to overcome them. Let's prove to them they totally underestimate our power. Let's distract them in a positive way and give them a piece of their own medicine.

I MUST ALWAYS BE OPEN TO THIS AS A MADMAN FOR GOOD!!!!

ENTRY #193

3/27/12 – 8:33am

ANOTHER MANIFESTO OF A MADMAN FOR GOOD

It's not only important to build up and motivate ourselves for the ideological and evolutionary battle in front of us, but to build up and motivate those around us as well. Our consciousness is no different in the same basic makeup or design as anybody else's. If we want to help raise consciousness and build people up with something they always had within them but might not have realized, we must ask ourselves why? We might say it's important to save the planet, make the economy fair for the working class, take better care of the poor or the environment; this is what the next step is all about, what we're going to do and how we're going to pull it off. We might know all this, but something still seems to be holding us back, even though we might be inches away from entering the race.

We must look inside ourselves and figure out if distractions are placed on us, or if we perpetuate them ourselves? Would they survive at all if we didn't buy into them? Is our faith in them the only thing keeping them alive?

I MUST CONTINUE TO LEARN AND BUILD AS A MADMAN FOR GOOD!!!!

ENTRY #194

3/27/12 – 8:44am

ANOTHER MANIFESTO OF A MADMAN FOR GOOD

Do the powerful say one person can't change the world because they want to distract us to the point that we're completely lobotomized to any other possibilities for change than the system they've created for us? Is it the rest of us who say one person can't change the world because we think the problem is too big, powerful and way to unforgiving for people who step out of line? Are both of these options completely separate from each other, do they serve the same purpose? Or are they completely dependent on each other, and can't survive without the other?

If the haves and have not's say one person can't change the world, is it true? Is it a way to keep people from rising up because they feel totally inadequate to the task? Or is it because one person can't change the world, but enough people together who see that way of thinking as horse shit, can?

One person can't change the world, but a group of "one persons" can. This is what we must remember and carry with us wherever we go; this is what we can use to motivate ourselves when times get rough. This might be our "why."

I MUST CONTINUE TO BUILD ON THIS AS A MADMAN FOR GOOD!!!!

ENTRY #195

3/27/12 – 8:56am

ANOTHER MANIFESTO OF A MADMAN FOR GOOD

If one person can't change the world but many "one persons" can, is it the same for ideas? Is it possible for one idea to change the world? If a lot of these "one ideas" were put together, would they have a bigger chance at making positive change? Or would there be too many hands in the pot and too many cooks in the kitchen?

A lot of us might feel and know in our hearts that something is wrong with society. Maybe we even talk about what is wrong, and we might even chuckle or laugh as a coping mechanism because it's so wrong. Maybe we are unaware of a solution. Maybe we're too wrapped up in surviving and living that we don't care enough to try and figure it out.

That's why when we talk, we really have to communicate, we might not know how and what to do, and neither might our friends; but the more we get together and keep positive thinking, positive change and consciousness raising on the front of our minds, the easier it will be to go about our lives from that point forward. Who knows, the idea or ideas that we have been waiting and/or searching for could just pop up, they might have been right in front of us the whole time.

I MUST INVESTIGATE AND KEEP SEARCHING FOR THIS AS A MADMAN FOR GOOD!!!!

ENTRY #196

3/28/12 – 8:08am

ANOTHER MANIFESTO OF A MADMAN FOR GOOD

When we unite, (not if, but when) we will have conversations, discussions, probably more than a few arguments; but once one we get used to a humanistic and accountable back and forth between each other, then the real work can begin. Is there a way we can use this humanistic, altruistic, empathetic and sympathetic attitude to achieve the goals we all want to achieve, but might never knew how to before? What actions should we take? What must we all do as a group to make sure the people at the top won't be able to distract us into oblivion anymore? What precautions must we take so we don't take one step forward and three steps back? What worries must we toss out so we don't get bogged down?

Once we unite and discuss the things that are on the tips of our tongues, we won't be afraid anymore of taking action. When we aren't afraid of saying what we really think because we won't be judged, we can put together some real solutions to the things we have always agreed needed fixing. Maybe we knew what do all along; we just needed the right motivation to push us there.

I MUST PREPARE AS A MADMAN FOR GOOD!!!!

ENTRY #197

3/28/12 – 8:19am

ANOTHER MANIFESTO OF A MADMAN FOR GOOD

If we have always felt solutions through direct action needed to be carried out, why haven't we done them yet? If we all think a certain system is stacked against us, why haven't we risen up to stop it yet? If we all know the education system is being privatized, being built more for profit motives than teaching kids the skills they need to carry on a productive society, why haven't we stood up and said enough? If we all know that the prison system is being privatized, being built only to generate profit and keep more people locked up cheaply for longer periods of time while inhibiting rehabilitation, instead of keeping recidivism rates low by educating and not segregating prisoners because profit and long sentences wouldn't be the first thing on their minds, why haven't we stood up and said enough? When we see instances of racial profiling and other racist acts perpetuated because old attitudes and emotions didn't disappear just because laws were passed years ago, when are we going to stand up and say enough is enough?

There are many other examples of things we all know are wrong and we all know could use fixing. So what are we waiting for?

I MUST STAY ETERNALLY VIGILANT AS A MADMAN FOR GOOD!!!!

ENTRY #198

3/28/12 – 8:31am

ANOTHER MANIFESTO OF A MADMAN FOR GOOD

If we are waiting for a miracle to fall out of the sky to fix all the problems in society, we might be waiting a lot longer than our human form will allow. We need to find that something within ourselves that will drive us to achieve what we always knew was possible, but just didn't realize it because we were distracted. We will unite sooner or later, but the key is that when we find our inner strength, we must share it with others because they are trying to find it too.

Once we are united through our universal human goals, we can start talking about the design of our plan for what must be done. Have we not figured out our plan yet because we've never fully come together before? Have the answers not popped up in our discussions or conversations because we haven't had the kinds of talks we should be having? When people say we shouldn't talk about politics or religion because things get out of hand, isn't that part of the problem? If we could discuss politics and religion humanely, then things might never get out of hand. If we were waiting for a miracle, this might be the closest we ever get.

I WILL ALWAYS CARRY ON AS A MADMAN FOR GOOD!!!!

ENTRY #199

3/28/12 – 8:42am

ANOTHER MANIFESTO OF A MADMAN FOR GOOD

We can move forward and we must move forward because being stagnant or moving backwards just isn't going to cut it anymore. We must unite, we must come up with solutions that benefit society as a whole, while at the same time showing the people at the top that they can't cant blind and distract us anymore.

We must show the "power brokers" as they try to entrench us in yet another battle amongst each other that we are going to catch them off-guard, because they don't know when we'll strike.

We must also show them that if they acquiesce to us, we will bring them to our side with open arms because they're still human; that's how we broaden our movement. We must also show the "elites" that if they still insist on gumming up the works and throwing monkey wrenches into the gears of human and emotional evolution, then they will be held to account and we will strike back against them.

We might not have to instill fear into the hearts of the have mores to get our point across if we frame it right; we might however come across some that are too stubborn and too ignorant for their own good and might get scared of the change we'll bring.

Something different doesn't have to be scary; it is just unknown. Let's delve into the unknown with positive thoughts and actions and see what happens.

I WILL ALWAYS STRIVE AND MOTIVATE AS A MADMAN FOR GOOD!!!!

ENTRY #200

3/28/12 – 8:53am

ANOTHER MANIFESTO OF A MADMAN FOR GOOD

To achieve positive change, it's going to take more work for some of us than others depending how far we've pushed it down the importance and priority scale. We must ask ourselves on a daily basis, what can I do today to effect positive change? What can I do today to raise my consciousness as well as others around me? What can I do today to sympathize and empathize with somebody I might completely disagree with? What can I do today to help bring people together, and what will make the difference in making it happen sooner rather than later? What ideas can we bring to the table, today, so the next time we're standing around with friends saying, "Jeez, we all want to do something, but what do we do" we have something more to answer than, I don't know?

We must ask ourselves these questions on a daily basis. We must stay eternally vigilant to the issues and problems surrounding us, and how they affect us all. We are in control of our own destiny, we do have the power. Let's show the "fat cats" at the top they can't keep us pacified and distracted anymore; they will see the full power of what they were trying to suppress and prevent very soon. Let's show them what people power is all about.

I MUST ALWAYS TAKE THIS CHALLENGE SERIOUSLY AS A MADMAN FOR GOOD!!!!

EPILOGUE

4/10/12 – 8:11am

ANOTHER MANIFESTO OF A MADMAN FOR GOOD

Coming together as a world, a country, a community and as a people is as important now as it's ever been. The entrenched powers that have been pushing the buttons and pulling the levers in the background for an extremely long time are finally emerging from the shadows and trying to legitimize and mainstream their actions. Things that were once thought secret, (even top secret) are being leaked or released for the world to see. All the information we need for the evolution of our revolution is right in front of us, down to the dirtiest, evilest and most despicable details of crimes and misfortunes. The question that might come up is that since the powers that be have kept this information secret for so many years, why now are they trying to legitimize it? If all these stories have come out about the CIA waterboarding, using "enhanced interrogation techniques" and how they're supposedly being used legally, haven't the CIA or any and all other spy agencies always used these methods? If breaking news happens about soldiers abusing prisoners, murdering entire villages, or just shooting random people because they felt like it, hasn't it happened before?

The point is that, all the information is out there dealing with darn near everything. Those of us at the top who push this information in the first place see all our misdeeds in the open and try to make excuses about their existence. Really horrible things like massacres and indiscriminately torturing children might be tried to be kept secret, but in the age of the internet, <u>ALL</u> information eventually becomes available to the public.

Accountability of public officials or any person in a position of power and authority is one of the basic tenets that will fix most of our problems; problems that we could definitely fix once we unite and come together. Think about it, we might disagree on gun rights and abortion, but we can all agree that mentally and violently disturbed people with violent pasts and/or presents shouldn't be able to kill a bunch of people indiscriminately because they bought a gun or got into the military without a background check. We could also agree that people not ready to have kids, shouldn't, because it vastly expands the welfare rolls and/or benefit cycles, or even worse, the kids aren't supported by their parents at all and then grow up to be detriments to society which nobody wants.

There are many things we don't agree on, but there are many things we can. If we are able to start from where we agree and then move into the subjects we don't, we will have a more healthy and productive life and might actually have a chance at solving some of the seemingly impossible to agree on issues.

We need to look at a different way to start the conversation. If we go at each other's throats by saying the other side is evil, criminal, socialist or fascist and will lead us down a path to destruction and doom, we won't get anywhere and will continue to be distracted by all the issues we shouldn't, which might be legitimate, but will stop our evolution in its tracks. We will stop trying to help each other and only live to tear the opposing side down because we think that's what will fix the problem at the top. We might be talking about major societal issues like the meaning of war and how a society should treat the lowest among us, but some of us can't remember that because we've been calling other people racist, homophobe, baby killer, socialist, communist, atheist, gay Nazis who are out to destroy all of humanity for their own personal gains.

Pause, isn't that what the people at the top cranking those cranks and pulling those levers want us to do? Isn't that what they've been striving for; to have us so distracted and fighting amongst each other that we won't see what they're up to? The "controllers" might be the ones laying down the importance about moral questions through the media or press releases, hell they might release their messages through PSA's that they can throw on the air as often or as fast as needed. When it comes down to it, the people at the top could care less about whether somebody can get married if they're gay, whether they have an abortion, or whether or not somebody gets a birth control handout from the government, they only use it as a smokescreen. They don't and won't care about any of it unless it affects their bottom line. They don't care about gay people if they aren't protesting specifically against them and affecting them. They don't care about abortion or birth control until an account refuses to do business with them or one of their major campaign contributor's cuts off their funding.

Maybe the key is turning it around on the "gatekeepers", (like they turned it around on us) and get them distracted and fighting fruitless battles amongst each other that won't get them ahead. We need to show them how we can keep them on their toes, and get them to flail around. Of course one question we must ask ourselves while all this is happening, is distracting them really fighting back and going on the offensive, or is it nothing more than stooping to their level? Is using their tactics against them hurting them more or hurting us more?

When we start thinking of actions we can take for the betterment of all society, there are all sorts of directions we could go. We could write letters, picket, protest, yell, scream and demand that our grievances be redressed. We could put on plays, paint pictures, make music, even do scientific research to root out the true meaning of our existence of why we are here. We could do just about anything. Our job, (and maybe the toughest one of all) is too not only find what will be the most effective way of moving forward, but also to find something we are passionate about that will drive us to achieve things we might never before have thought possible. We all serve a purpose; we all can make this world a better place for all of us. I know a lot of this might sound like high-falootin talk about one "madman's" dream to save the world; well, it might be. The point though, isn't the world worth saving, isn't it worth fighting for? All the hopes and dreams we have for how the world might be peaceful one day, why shouldn't we work to make them come true?

We must realize the day we've been waiting for is upon us, and the time for action is now. We can't wait any longer for the world to fix itself of the problems we know would be elementary to solve as long the world got its collective head out of its ass. We must be the change we want to see. If there is something the military does that we don't like or structures something in a certain way that feeds a vicious cycle of mutually assured destruction, we must stand up and let the people controlling it know how we feel.

If health care companies act purely out of a profit motive without giving second thought to the patients they are supposed to be treating, we must stand up and say why it's wrong. If the prison system is run so much from a profit motive (for a company or a government) that laws get harsher, sentences get longer and jail populations grow and grow and grow with no end in sight, we must stand up and say enough is enough. If there are problems with the way humans treat each other, we need to make sure we remember how we ourselves like to be treated and that we have the same basic needs as everyone else.

How do we get the ball rolling on all this, maybe by realizing a lot of us have the same pent up feelings about domination and control? This is a way to start uniting around a common goal, because we'll know that humanism and accountability in all things and in all people is the key to that unification. Sure, we must learn when to compromise and when to fight; but before we can get to that point we must get past the stupid and meaningless distractions that hold us back from the place we all want to get to. It doesn't matter what somebody looks like, what their beliefs are or who they happen to fall in love with; what matters is what's in their heart. What matters is getting to the point where a light bulb goes off in our head and we say wait, we all want the same thing. Why am I making fun of you or demeaning you for being gay when we all want to find love? Why am I okay with making war, when all I want is peace?

We must think about when to compromise and when to fight. We must remember what's really important to us, might be also really important to that person over there that is marginalized for not being what society thinks they should be. We must all stand up and do our part in our own way for the betterment of society. The problems we all face are huge, and have been ingrained in our psyches for generations. It is going to take a multi-pronged attack to get the job done to fix it. It's about all of us making a contribution and putting our strengths forward to help out the cause of raising our collective consciousness so we can positively evolve as a human species. We must keep moving forward, and even though the journey is long and fraught with peril, it's a lot more easily traveled in a large and cohesive human family then all alone (the unification we all crave but sometimes can't put words to).

All of this is possible, the world's problems are fixable no matter how tough they might seem. Sometimes their difficulty is just a smokescreen to make them seem like a much more insurmountable opponent than they really are, a distraction you might say; kind of like the distractions that keep us down, the ones we feed into only causing themselves to become stronger and to keep us down even longer. And on and on and on the cycle goes of never-ending pain and suffering of us never thinking things will ever get better. Well my friends, do you think it's time we break that cycle? Do you think we are ready to break out of the mold we presently find ourselves in? Do you think it's time we all take action and see what can happen and what we can accomplish if we all work together?

It can be that time if we want it to be. We can work with one another to shake off this funk we are in. Distractions can only grab onto us if we let them. Let's shake them off, and let's get to work saving the world, our country, our city, our community, our family, our friends and ourselves. Let's show these bastards at the top who is really in charge and who should be making the decisions from now on.

We can change ourselves, our community, our country and our planet if we set out to do it. We can be the people we have been waiting for. Let's get to work!!!!

I DEDICATE MY LIFE AS A MADMAN FOR GOOD TO DOING WHATEVER I CAN, WHENEVER I CAN AND WHEREVER I CAN TO RAISE EVERYBODYS CONSCIOUSNESS INCLUDING MY OWN, SO WE ALL CAN EVOLVE, SO WE ALL CAN LIVE!!!!

www.ingramcontent.com/pod-product-compliance
Lightning Source LLC
LaVergne TN
LVHW011230080426
835509LV00005B/412